Deploying Linux on the Desktop

Deploying Linux on the Desktop

Edward Haletky

ELSEVIER
DIGITAL
PRESS

Amsterdam · Boston · Heidelberg · London · New York · Oxford
Paris · San Diego · San Francisco · Singapore · Sydney · Tokyo

Elsevier Digital Press
30 Corporate Drive, Suite 400, Burlington, MA 01803, USA
Linacre House, Jordan Hill, Oxford OX2 8DP, UK

∞ Recognizing the importance of preserving what has been written, Elsevier prints its books on acid-free paper whenever possible.

Library of Congress Cataloging-in-Publication Data
Application Submitted.

ISBN: 1-55558-328-8

British Library Cataloguing-in-Publication Data
A catalogue record for this book is available from the British Library.

For information on all Elsevier Digital Press publications
visit our Web site at www.books.elsevier.com

Transferred to Digital Printing 2009

To Dad, who always told us to "Stay smart."
(April 10, 1938–October 8, 2004)

Contents

Acknowledgments

I would like to thank my wife Romy and my extended family for their ongoing support throughout the writing of this book. Romy gave me the time to work on this book by keeping the "honey-do" lists to a minimum and encouraging me to continue to write. Romy also donated her doctoral thesis as the best test of many of the document tools available for Linux; pages of her work are within this book. Thank you, Romy; I deeply appreciate your support.

Furthermore, I would like to thank my friends Chris and Pat for reviewing the chapters for technical faults as they rolled off the word processor, and for keeping me on my toes with their insightful questions and suggestions. Many thanks! In addition, I would like to thank Pat for providing part of a chapter on the iPAQ; he has one, whereas I only have a Palm device.

Last, I wish to acknowledge my friends, coworkers, and family for their support and encouragement.

Much more than a jumpstart, this book is my recipe for building a usable Linux corporate desktop that moves far beyond migration to Linux and into the concept of integration. This book endeavors to meet the challenge of integrating Linux into the corporate environment with a minimized learning curve and no loss of functionality. This book presents the tools necessary to build toward integration, as well as the costs and support considerations that arise from the use of Linux on the desktop. Included is my personal recipe for building my laptop (see Chapter 13).

About this Book

Covering Red Hat Enterprise Linux 3 and 4, SuSE Enterprise Linux 9, and Mandrake Linux, this book provides the necessary tools that will allow its readers to use Linux within a Microsoft-centric network environment. It is an invaluable reference regarding the creation of an integrated Linux corporate desktop!

E-mail address: books@astroarch.com

Web site: http://www.astroarch.com/~elh/books

The Requirements

Looking at the world of the desktop computer, you see a myriad of solutions ranging from Microsoft Windows 98 and other versions, to Macintosh computers of all types, to Linux, the new rising star. While we know that Microsoft Windows and Macintosh have been competitors, more and more eyes are investigating Linux as a solution to rising IT costs. Even so, many are unwilling, or unprepared, to take the plunge and use this open-source operating system. So more information is needed, a readily available resource that both addresses the issues inherent in using Linux in a non-Linux-centric desktop world and provides an information source for IT managers and those system administrators with a clear understanding of Linux basics.

It is necessary to describe the complete scope of this book based on desktop-user requirements. These requirements will dictate the questions to be answered by each subsequent chapter of this book, and stem from two basic questions:

1. Is Linux ready for real use as a desktop?

2. Is Linux ready to be used as a corporate desktop?

The easy answer to both is yes. Linux is ready, but the matter is much more complex than that. Let us look at two distinct scenarios and try to further refine our answer.

The first scenario consists of using Linux as a replacement for all existing machines, from file servers to desktops: a homogenous Linux solution that will not interact with any other types of systems. The second scenario consists of a heterogeneous solution, in which Linux may act as a desktop, server, and so on. While the first scenario is a dream many Linux developers have, the second scenario is a more honest world view.

Scenario One is a rousing affirmative. Everything works as expected for the corporate environment.

Scenario Two is a golf-clap affirmative. Everything will work, but it requires more of a mixed-mode desktop, which uses Linux as the operating system and possibly tools such as Wine and VMware to complete the interoperability requirements.

With Scenario Two firmly in mind, we should look at Linux as an enabling tool that has some native applications, as well as at tools to use non-native applications that may have no Linux equivalent. Each chapter looks at the desktop from this world view and answers the questions presented to an administrator who must solve the problems of maintaining a heterogeneous environment that interoperates successfully, and identify the cost and benefits the administrator can bring to the IT manager who makes those decisions.

While this book can be viewed as a list of Frequently Asked Questions (FAQ), a collection of how-to documents, or a list of power tools or hacks I will answer the IT manager's question, "What is the cost of using Linux on the corporate desktop?" as well as the system administrator's question, "What is involved in implementing Linux on a corporate desktop?" To come up with this information, we must first visit the requirements of a corporate desktop.

The list of requirements has been taken from my own experiences in using a common desktop within a corporate environment on a laptop that must be useable by all described user types. We have approached this list to fulfill the needs of three different user types:

1.   Telecommuter—Tools and requirements to set up a home office desktop

2.   Corporate office user—Tools and requirements to set up an effective Linux desktop in the corporate office or cubicle

3.   Road warriors—Tools and requirements to set up a useful Linux environment on a laptop

The requirements are broken out for these environments by classification of tools. The order of the requirements, and hence the chapters, takes the reader from the basics of connectivity through the final touches of more esoteric desktop tools. It should be noted that a broad stroke of the brush has been used with our lists of requirements; your environment may not need every tool discussed and may need other tools not discussed herein.

Listing your requirements before you delve into setting up and integrating a Linux desktop is extremely important, as it will set the tone for your method of integration. It will also give you a chance to plan your approach and any possible outlay of money needed to finish the integration.

Consider the following example: Your corporate environment uses Microsoft Office, yet you do not need Access, Visio, or FrontPage. However, use of e-mail, Word, and Excel is paramount. In addition, you have network printers as well as Windows-based file servers. Everyone in the office has a PalmOS device of some type. Web content is generally simple, with shared Word or Excel documents available. Last, IRC is the interoffice communication tool of choice.

Looking at the above example it appears that requirements are the following:

Word

Excel

Exchange

Printing

File sharing

PalmOS Desktop and HotSync

Web browser with Word/Excel plug-ins

IRC

This book covers the following requirements, of which the above is a subset. While your requirements may not be so limited, these are a typical core list and make a good example of how to use this book to determine what you will need. Once you have defined your requirements, you can then peruse the appropriate chapters and determine which apply to your desktop environment. Each chapter will be laid out in an easy-to-read question-and-answer format, which will aid in determining which questions you should ask when coming up with requirements.

CHAPTERS

Instant Messaging

Peer-to-Peer Video Sharing

7. Terminal Emulators and Server Clients

Legacy System CLI Access

Windows Terminal Services

Citrix Metaframe

8. Home Office Tools

Palm Desktop

Documents-To-Go

Image Sync to PDA

Home Finance Programs

QuickBooks

Digital Camera Link

9. SPAM and Virus Protections

SPAM Filtering

E-Mail Virus Protection

Scanning Machines for Viruses

Choosing your requirements in advance gives you a clear understanding of what you will need on your Linux desktop. It also gives you an opportunity to reflect on the use of these tools. In some cases, you may find you only need tools in their most basic form, while in others you may need more advanced features. For example, a Word document might be your format of choice, and the only advanced feature you use is the grammar checker; another office may require that change control and tracking be used with every document. These extra requirements can change which tool you decide to install on your Linux desktop.

So our example would change to look something like the following, as each tool is considered and its feature use is understood:

Word—grammar/spell-checker

Excel—graphing capability

Exchange—single user and group accounts

Printing—Windows-based printer access

File sharing—Windows-based file sharing

Palm OS Desktop and HotSync—Documents-To-Go

Web browser with Word/Excel plug-ins

IRC

Understanding how the tools are used in your current environment will aid is determining what you need to do on a Linux system to achieve the same results, and whether or not your new Linux desktops must be changed to reflect how things are handled on your central servers. Such knowledge could even affect your security settings.

Finally, advance planning will also help you understand the training that may be required as people switch from one operating system to another. It must be understood in advance that seemingly equivalent tools on Linux do not behave in exactly the same way as the tools in the Microsoft environment. The installation and configuration of such tools are often radically different not only between Linux and Microsoft, but also between various Linux distributions. This book will concentrate on Red Hat Enterprise Linux version 3 Workstation (RHEL3 or RHEL3-WS). Wherever possible, we will also look at the SuSE, Mandrake, and Fedora distributions of Linux.

In summary: You can use the chapter list to create a list of the tools you will need in advance. Make note of any specific features in the tools you select that will be required either by local system settings, corporate use guidelines, or security requirements. Last, make sure you understand the learning that will be required as you move to your new Linux environment.

2

Virtual Private Network (VPN) Connectivity

A growing number of road warriors need to connect into the corporate environment using a Virtual Private Network (VPN). This chapter will address three of the possible methods for connecting to the corporate LAN using Linux. It will not cover setting up modems, but will cover setting up the necessary software to implement VPN. The goal is not to provide a detailed guide on which to choose, but instead to provide the practical knowledge of how to implement the necessary components and their associated costs.

2.1   How Do I Connect Using PPTP?

PPTP (Point to Point Tunneling Protocol) requires adding modules to your kernel, as well as a specialized setup using pptpconfig and other necessary system modifications to implement the PPTP protocol. http://pptpclient.sourceforge.net is an extremely good Web site that provides an excellent reference for PPTP on Linux. While we will not discuss every distribution, the steps are generally the same for all. Since using PPTP requires root access, it is not a bad idea to use a program such as *sudo* or similar tool to control access to this critical component or to use the PPTP service setup with *pptp-command*.

2.1.1   RHEL3

When installing PPTP into RHEL3, you will need to add modules into the kernel to add the required encryption. Once these modules are added, it is just a case of defining everything properly in the configuration files and then launching the PPTP configuration with the launch tools. As an added bonus the current PPTP modules have been compiled to use Dynamic Kernel Module Support (DKMS). DKMS aids you when the kernel is upgraded, as you do not need to remember to recompile your kernel modules by hand. The recompilation will happen automatically, which will decrease support issues when kernels are upgraded for security or bugfix reasons. DKMS will also provide a simpler way to distribute third party modules to each host. Below are the steps necessary to install PPTP using the DKMS form of the modules. Also note that this step install DKMS which is in RPM format. There are other formats for other versions of Linux available.

```
# rpm -ivh ppp-2.4.3-0.cvs_20040527.1.i386.rpm pptp-linux--
1.4.0-1.i386.rpm pptp-php-gtk-20040102-rc1.i386.rpm dkms-1.12-
1.noarch.rpm kerneel_ppp_mppe-0.0.3-1dkms.noarch.rpm
...
DKMS: Add Completed.

Preparing kernel 2.4.21-15.0.4.EL for module build:
(This is not compiling a kernel, only preparing kernel symbols)
Storing current .config to be restored when complete
Running Red Hat preparation routine
...
Building module:
...
DKMS: Build Completed.
...
DKMS: Install Completed.
# service dkms_autoinstaller start
# chkconfig dkms_autoinstaller on
# modprobe -v ppp_mppe
# lsmod | grep ppp
ppp_mppe                  13816    0   (unused)
ppp_generic               24436    0   [ppp_mppe]
slhc                       6672    0   [ppp_generic]
# pptpconfig
-Or-
# pptp-command
```

There are two ways to configure PPTP, and they are independent of each other: *pptpconfig* is a graphical tool, and *pptp-command* is a character cell mechanism. *pptp-command* also has a service that can start at boot time after your network comes up (*pptpconfig* does not have this ability). Both must be run as root . pptpconfig on RHEL3 will automatically ask for the root password when launched, while pptp-command requires the user to be logged in as root to launch. Before using pptp-command or even pptpconfig it is best to check with the corporate security policies as

Figure 2.1
*Server information
for PPTP
configuration.*

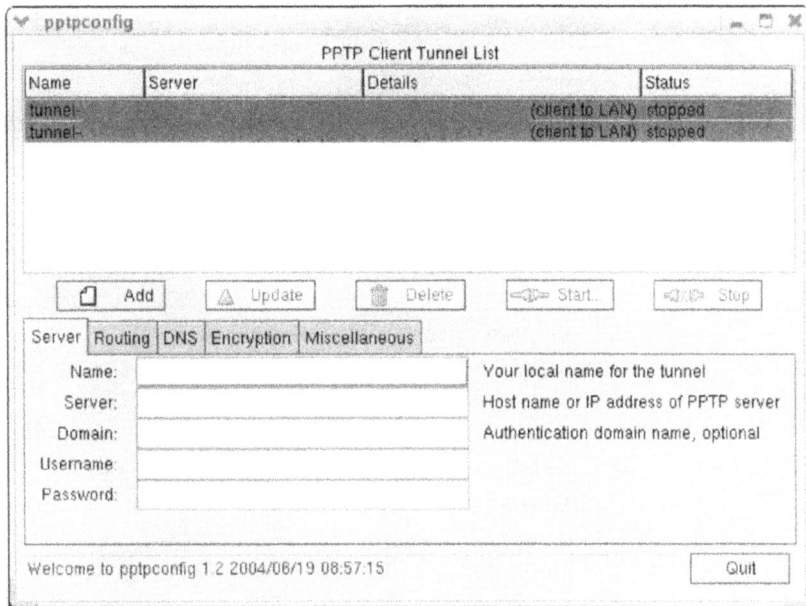

automatic logins to a VPN may not be allowed. While certainly conve-
nient, pptp-command is not for the faint of heart and not covered herein.
When running *pptpconfig*, you will configure using the following screens
(Figures 2.1, 2.2, and 2.3):

Figure 2.1 illustrates the server information box. You will need to fill in
your server information as well as Routing, DNS, Encryption, and Miscellaneous information.

Figure 2.2 illustrates encryption choices. For example, my servers
require the displayed items to be checked for encryption.

Figure 2.3 illustrates the miscellaneous options.

2.1.2 Other Versions

It is interesting to note that the Gentoo version of Linux contains the necessary tools to use PPTP, while most other mainstream versions of Linux do
not contain the tools by default.

2.2 How Do I Connect Using IPSec?

IPSec (IP Secure) uses the Openswan package to implement the IPSec stack
and to connect to an Openswan server on the corporate network. The

Figure 2.2
*Encryption
information for
PPTP
configuration.*

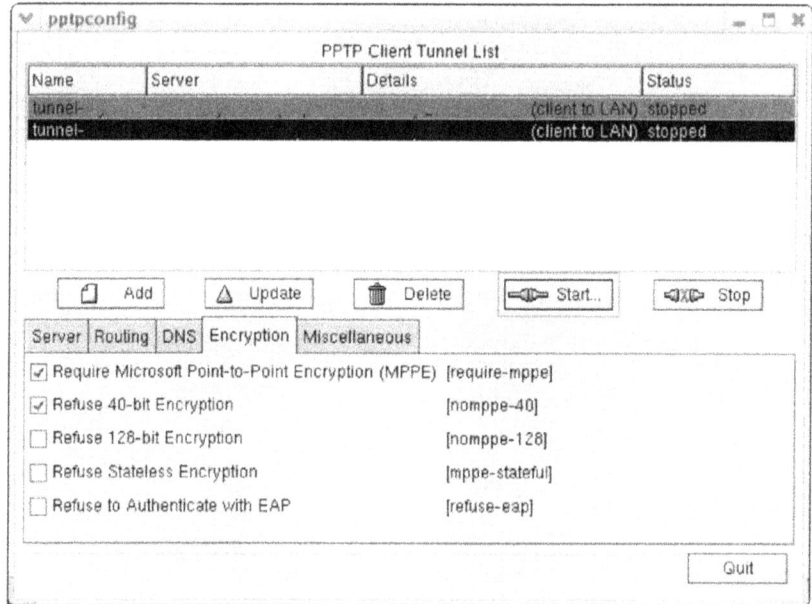

Figure 2.3
*Miscellaneous
information for
PPTP
configuration.*

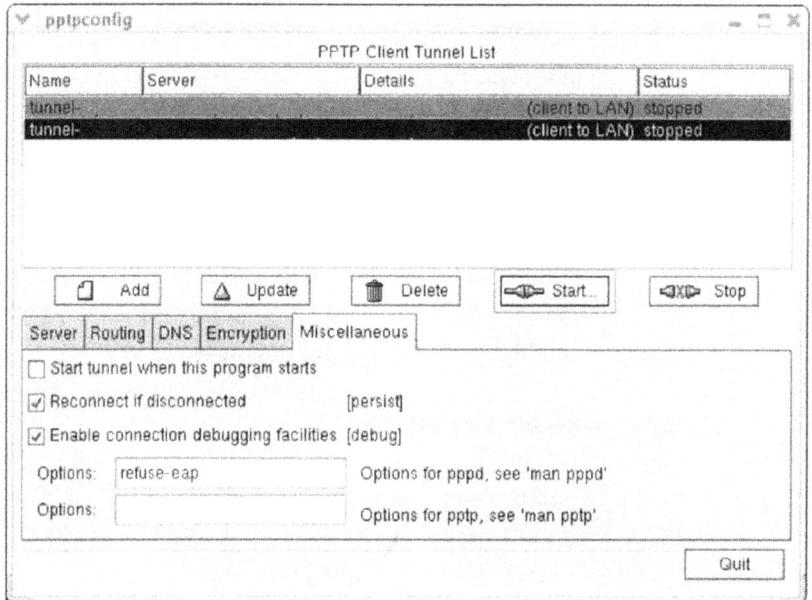

implementation of Open-swan is similar across most Linux distributions; http://www.openswan.org provides an excellent Openswan implementation guide. NAT Traversal support (NAT-T) often requires patching the kernel. In general, version 2.6 kernels will already contain the IPSec and dependent modules, while some 2.4 kernels will need to compile the module into your kernel. While IPSec use is growing there is a fair amount of incompatibility between servers and often requires a specialized client to use.

2.2.1 RHEL (Red Hat Enterprise Linux)

Openswan does not install on RHEL3-WS as the IPSec module has dependency issues. However, IPSec support is part of RHEL3 and RHEL4. Refer to http://www.redhat.com/docs/manuals/enterprise/RHEL-?-Manual/security-guide/s1-vpn-ipsec.html, where the ? is either 3 or 4 depending on your release, to get specific installation and setup instructions. In addition, http://www.cs.helsinki.fi/u/mikkila/docs/linux-avaya-vsu.html#native_config provides an easy to use installation discussion on IPsec support in RHEL3 or RHEL4. If you need NAT-T support, however, you will need to recompile your kernel completely with a patch that will void your RHEL warranty.

2.2.2 Fedora

Fedora Core 2 or 3 (kernel v2.6) already contains an IPSec module, without NAT-T support. Following the instructions at http://www.cs.helsinki.fi/u/mikkila/docs/linux-avaya-vsu.html#native_config and even those for RHEL3 and RHEL4 depending on your release of Fedora will ais greatly. Once more NAT-T support will need to be compiled into your kernel.

2.2.3 VMware

VMware workstation is a for-fee ($199) program that provides a virtual machine in which you can run an implementation of Microsoft Windows. This will allow you to use the Microsoft-provided dial-up and VPN tools to connect to the corporate LAN. This is the most compatible VPN method, and includes the ability to cache domain credentials easily. Setting up a VPN in VMware could be as simple as creating a new network adapter or as complex as installing specialized software.

To allow the Linux host access to your VPN running within VMware, you must configure your VMware virtual machine to act as a router, either using Internet Connection Sharing or some other proxy/router software. Use of these tools may be strictly monitored or even virtually impossible to use, due to existing required security, VPN software, or even your corporate written security policy. Also, confirm that these tools are allowed on Microsoft systems before proceeding. Once one of these methods is in use, you can change your Linux default route to your VMware virtual machine's address, set a few other items such as DNS servers, and you are good to go. If, however, you do not have root access to your system, you will need to depend on these being properly set for use, using as many different tools as there are versions of Linux:

RHEL3: redhat-config-network

Mandrake: drakeconf

SuSE: yast2

Fedora/RHEL4: system-config-network

2.3   How Do I Connect Using SSH Tunneling?

But what about SSH? Does the secure shell provide a method to tunnel? The answer is yes, but outside of Linux and modern Macintosh computers I have not seen it in wide use. However, before you can use SSH tunneling, you must have a valid connection to a network, and this is where other VPN solutions may come into play. One advantage of SSH is that any network connection can be used to start up the tunneling. Once again, you will need root access, so the *sudo* command is invaluable. We will not delve into SSH, as there are other resources available for this technology.

2.4   Wireless and Other Network Devices

The complexities of modern wireless devices deserve a mention. Many of the slower wireless devices work out of the box on Linux. These devices are following the Wireless-B standards. However, the modern Wireless-G devices (except for Prism-based Wireless-G devices) need help from an open source project, and note that the Prism drivers are not available with some older kernels. The Ndiswrapper project (http://ndiswrapper.source-forge.net) will load a Microsoft NT Ndis driver into a Linux kernel so that modern Wireless-G devices will work. The NT Ndis driver will read the Windows based wireless device driver copied to the Linux system from its Media and use this to control the device. This helps the road warriors. As an example, we have a recipe for configuring a LinkSys Wireless-G PCI and PCMCIA device:

```
# tar -xzf ndiswrapper-0.9.tar.gz
# cd ndiswrapper-0.9
# make install
# mkdir /usr/local/linksys.WMP54G (PCI)
copy the driver files bcmwl5.* to /usr/local/linksys.WMP54G
from the CDROM
- OR -
# mkdir /usr/local/linksys.WPC54G (PCMCIA)
copy the driver files bcmwl5.* to /usr/local/linksys.WPC54G
from the CDROM

# ndiswrapper -l # check for any existing drivers
# ndiswrapper -i /usr/local/linksys.WPC54G/bcmwl5.inf # install
driver
# ndiswrapper -l # check to see if installed
# edit modules.conf to set add 'alias wlan0 ndiswrapper'
Configure WLAN0
```

Once your WLAN0 device is configured using one of the aforementioned network configuration tools, you can use the Wireless-G device quite easily. There is also DriverLoader, a third-party product from Linuxant (www.linuxant.com). DriverLoader is very similar to NdisWrapper and costs $19.95.

Both NdisWrapper and DriverLoader use the drivers provided with the wireless device in use so you will need the device media when installing these tools.

Also, some ethernet devices must have new drivers built to gain access to all their full features. One family of such devices is from Broadcom. While the standard tg3 driver works, it has no facility to apply options to the driver to control the speed, duplex, and so forth. Hence, you may need to recompile the BCM5700 driver to handle these options. You can easily fit this driver and the NdisWrapper driver into DKMS so that you do not need to recompile either driver by hand when security and other updates to kernels occur. While the following steps work for RHEL3, they work equally well with the versions of Linux I have tested.

2.4.1   BCM5700 Driver via DKMS

We are working with Broadcom 5700 (BCM5700) driver v7.1.9e. I used the following procedure to add this into DKMS as root. While there may be an easier way, this method works quite well and allows for the building of the appropriate BCM5700 driver that *will* give me GigE speeds, as necessary.

```
# mkdir /usr/src/kernel_bcm5700-7.1.9e
# cd /usr/src/kernel_bcm5700-7.1.9e
# tar —xzf bcm5700-7.1.9e.tgz
Create a file named dkms.conf with the following contents:
PACKAGE_VERSION="7.1.9e"

# Items below here should not have to change with each driver
version
PACKAGE_NAME="kernel_bcm5700"
BUILT_MODULE_NAME[0]="bcm5700"
DEST_MODULE_LOCATION[0]="/kernel/drivers/net/"
AUTOINSTALL="yes"
REMAKE_INITRD="no"

# These are used for 2.4 kernels only
MAKE[0]="make all"
CLEAN="make clean"
```

Then run the following commands:

```
# dkms add —m kernel_bcm5700 —v 7.1.9e
# service dkms_autoinstaller start
```

2.4.2 NdisWrapper via DKMS

NdisWrapper can also be added into the DKMS framework quite easily.
Actually, it is easier than the BCM5700 driver discussed previously, as no
special build script is necessary. These brief instructions will do all you
need. DKMS requires that the install module path start with /kernel, so you
will need to change the Makefile according to the following instructions.

```
# mkdir /usr/src/kernel_ndiswrapper
# cd /usr/src/kernel_ndiswrapper
# tar —xzf ndiswrapper-0.9.tar.gz
# mv ndiswrapper-0.9/* .; rmdir ndiswrapper-0.9
Edit driver/Makefile to change Install path from 'misc' to
'kernel/drivers/net'.
Create a file named dkms.conf with the following contents:
PACKAGE_VERSION="0.9"

# Items below here should not have to change with each driver
version
PACKAGE_NAME="kernel_ndiswrapper"
BUILT_MODULE_NAME[0]="ndiswrapper"
BUILD_MODULE_LOCATION[0]="driver"
```

```
DEST_MODULE_LOCATION[0]="/kernel/drivers/net/"
AUTOINSTALL="yes"
REMAKE_INITRD="no"


# These are used for 2.4 kernels only
MAKE[0]="make all"
CLEAN="make clean"
```

Then run the following commands:

```
# dkms add —m kernel_ndiswrapper —v 0.9
# service dkms_autoinstaller start
```

2.5 The Cost

Are there any hidden costs to using Linux as a VPN platform? There are dollar costs as well as support costs associated with using these tools. The dollar costs are related to the purchase of hardware and the necessary software to implement VPN. Since modern VPN clients may also require biometric dongles or cards, their costs are no different than any other system. The software costs could be very different between systems however. If you are using generic tools then there are minimal costs unless VMware is to be used.

Table 2.1 shows the costs involved.

Table 2.1 *Costs of using Linux as a VPN Platform*

Software	Support Level	Fee	Support Fee
PPTP	OpenSource	NA	NA
OpenSWAN/IPsec	OpenSource	NA	NA
VMware	Web-based/Phone	$199	Free for 90 days
NdisWrapper	OpenSource	NA	NA
DriverLoader	E-mail/Phone	$19.95	NA
DKMS	OpenSource	NA	NA
SSH Tunneling	OpenSource	NA	NA

2.6   Support Issues

There are however some pretty major support issues when using VPN tools
on Linux, not the least of them is the recompilation of your kernel for
NAT-T support, which will void your warranty on your system. Actually,
any recompilation or modification of your kernel will void such a warranty.
The addition of modules will not do void your warranty, but you may need
to disable their use to fully debug a system, as the specific modules will not
be supportable.

After such a strong statement why would anyone use these tools?
Because the opensource communities are very active, capable, and provide
excellent support for their modules. In addition, DKMS implementations
will decrease the number of support calls and allow Corporate IT depart-
ments more control over what tools are currently in use.

3

Office

A major part of using Linux as a corporate desktop is achieving compatibility with the Microsoft Office tool suite. This chapter contains information on Linux tools that equate with Microsoft Office products such as Exchange, Word, Excel, PowerPoint, Access, FrontPage, and Publisher. First, we will cover Linux-only solutions, then solutions using Wine, and, finally, VMware. We have also included in this chapter Visio and printing services for Windows-based network printers. While this chapter discusses many features of printing, we do not discuss its implementation; it is expected that the reader will have some knowledge of the CUPS or Berkeley Print subsystems.

When testing to see whether the available tools will work for your situation, it is best to have on hand a complex document of the appropriate type available to perform these tests. When I perform this test, I look for on-screen differences that will lead to formatting issues in any of the tools presented. For this test I used a dissertation document that includes images and complex templates; for PowerPoint, I included movies and other objects.

Even though this chapter appears to state mostly the limitations with Linux tools, it should not be interpreted as such. Linux tools will always be behind the development curve, since Microsoft is not assisting in this effort. Also, I should remind you that if you are using a homogenous Linux solution, these tools are not issues.

3.1   Word

One of the most widely used formats for document preparation and sharing is Microsoft Word, and Linux has quite a few tools to read and edit such documents. Here is a description of some of the most widely known tools.

3.1.1   OpenOffice

OpenOffice is the most commonly suggested tool for editing Word documents. Specifically you would use the OpenOffice Suite's *oowriter* tool. You can run *oowriter* from the command line or select its icon from the toolbar.

OpenOffice does have problems with Word documents. At the very least you may experience formatting issues (i.e., incorrect page numbering and page alignment; see Figures 3.1 and 3.2). At the most, graphics may not appear where you had originally placed them, or sections of text may be misplaced. This disconnect is because some of the more esoteric features of Word do not work with OpenOffice, which is by its nature behind the development curve.

Due to the different fonts available and issues with page numbering, the visual format of the document can appear skewed. You may wish to choose one system upon which the final format will be performed.

3.1.2   StarOffice

StarOffice is similar to OpenOffice, but is a for-fee product from Sun Microsystems. Actually, StarOffice used to be much more integrated as a desktop in

Figure 3.1
*Comparison
between Word and
oowriter.*

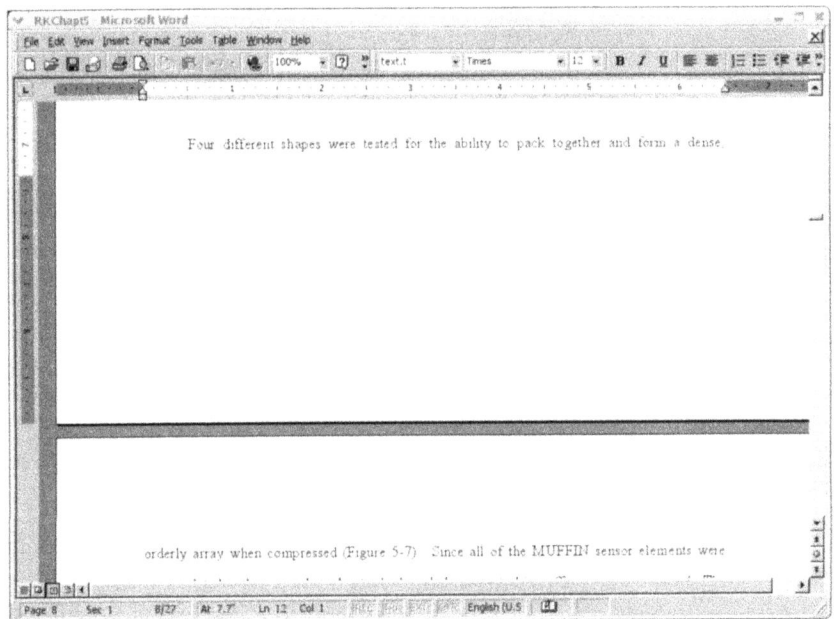

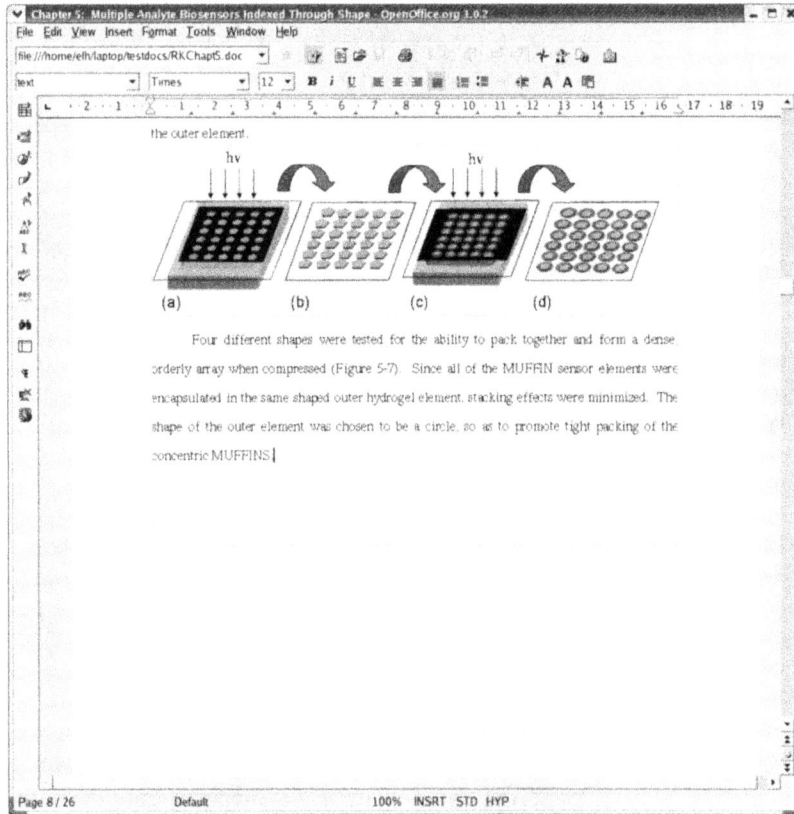

Figure 3.2
*Another
comparison
between Word and
oowriter: page
alignment.*

its "free" days; now, it is a drop-in replacement for OpenOffice. Since it is for-fee, you gain technical support through the product developers.

StarOffice is invoked using the command *soffice*. Star Office has issues similar to those of OpenOffice in dealing with page formatting. I suggest testing with the documents involved first, as the issues with page number-ing and different fonts on each system (Linux vs. Windows) will change how the documents look.

3.1.3 CrossOver Office

CrossOver Office allows the user to install a version of Microsoft Word into the system and use this instead of a native Linux tool. While in most cases this will alleviate the need for separate tools, many of the Word plug-ins may not install or even work, because the underlying Wine sub-system used by CrossOver Office is still under development (even though it's a stable release).

In the case of spell-checking, you will want to ensure that multiple languages are installed, since the spell-checker often asks me for the Italian language for some unknown reason. Perhaps it is the technical nature of my writing.

3.1.4 AbiWord

We should mention AbiWord as well as the others. It is a very nice editor that will read some Microsoft Word formats, yet its inability to save in a usable Microsoft Word document format is very limiting and frustrating when trying to interoperate.

3.2   Excel

One of the most widely used formats for spreadsheet preparation and sharing is Microsoft Excel. Linux has quite a few tools to read and edit spreadsheet files. Here is a short list of some of the most widely known tools.

There are several tools available to edit Excel files, just as there are for Word documents.

3.2.1 OpenOffice

OpenOffice editor for Excel is invoked using the *oocalc* command, or from the system menu or panel. OpenOffice is highly recommended as a way to manipulate Excel files on Linux, and is very good. However, as with the Word Document editor for OpenOffice, there are also issues with *oocalc*. These issues revolve around Excel's interpretation of formulas in files saved using OpenOffice (see Figures 3.3 and 3.4).

3.2.2 StarOffice

StarOffice is a for-fee version of OpenOffice that has taken a different development path but behaves in a similar fashion. The different development paths have not changed the behavior very much; StarOffice suffers from the same issues of chart and diagram placements, as well as Excel's display of cells with formulas from StarOffice. (It should be noted that although the cell formula saved, *=(B60)*2*, did not appear properly within Excel, it does appear properly in OpenOffice and StarOffice.)

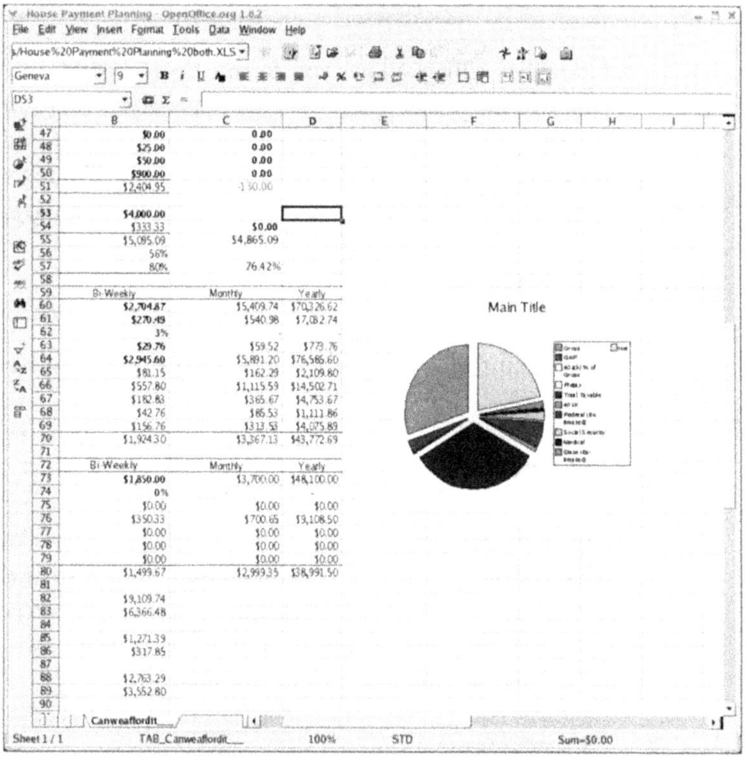

Figure 3.3
*Comparison
between Excel and
oocalc.*

Figure 3.3
*Comparison
between Excel and
oocalc.*

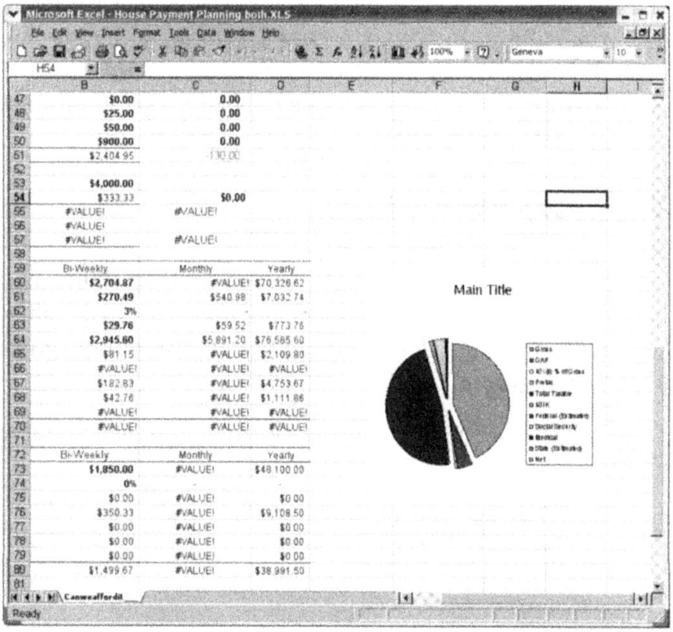

Figure 3.4
*Another
comparison
between Excel and
oocalc.*

3.2.3   **CrossOver Office**

CrossOver Office allows you to run Excel directly on your Linux desktop. The advantages are great; the only drawback is that some of the Excel plug-ins will not work. The underlying Wine system (used to emulate a Windows machine) does not have a 100-percent Windows implementation, so some of these untested plug-ins could crash the program.

3.3   **PowerPoint**

PowerPoint files, as with Word and Excel files, can be edited using similar tools.

3.3.1   **OpenOffice**

OpenOffice's *ooimpress* tool is used to edit and view PowerPoint files. Complex and simple files can be edited and viewed with ease. There are issues with display sometimes the Linux fonts will exceed the page frame, although they would not exceed it on a Windows machine. However, linked video is not a part of OpenOffice.

3.3.2   **StarOffice**

StarOffice can view and edit PowerPoint files with ease. However, it suffers the same formatting errors as OpenOffice. Figure 3.6 shows a very subtle difference between them. This difference demonstrates the different formatting that can occur. Note the name 'Grant' on the lower right is diffferent between PowerPoint and OpenOffice.

3.3.3   **CrossOver Office**

CrossOver Office will run Microsoft PowerPoint within the Linux environment using the Wine emulator. However, plug-ins may not work within this emulation environment, nor will most of the esoteric features of PowerPoint.

Our test included linked video, images, and links, which all displayed as expected.

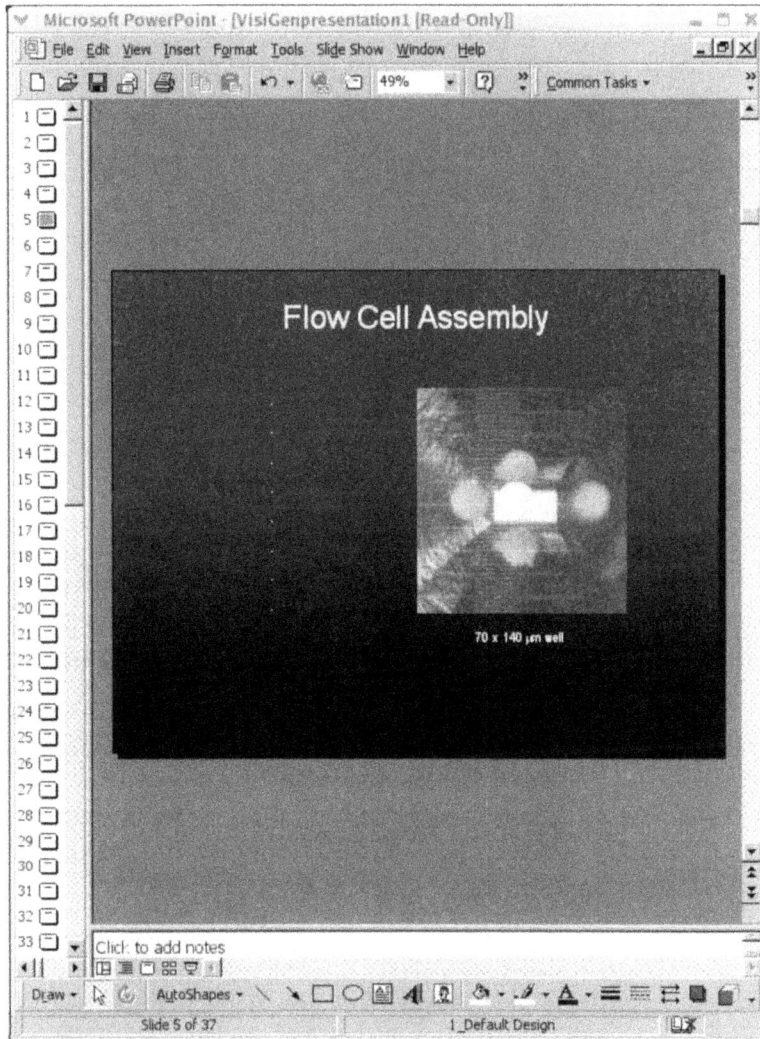

3.4 Access Database

Access, unlike the other Microsoft Office tools, does not have an immediate Linux equivalent. In general, you will need to use a helper program to create and manipulate tables in an Access database. Since database data is generally accessed through a third-party tool or program, an access tool is not always needed; however, you do need a back-end database. The most common databases are MySQL and PostgreSQL. Using MDB Tools, you can export your Access databases into MySQL, Oracle, Sybase, and Postgr-

Figure 3.6
*The PowerPoint
Movie.*

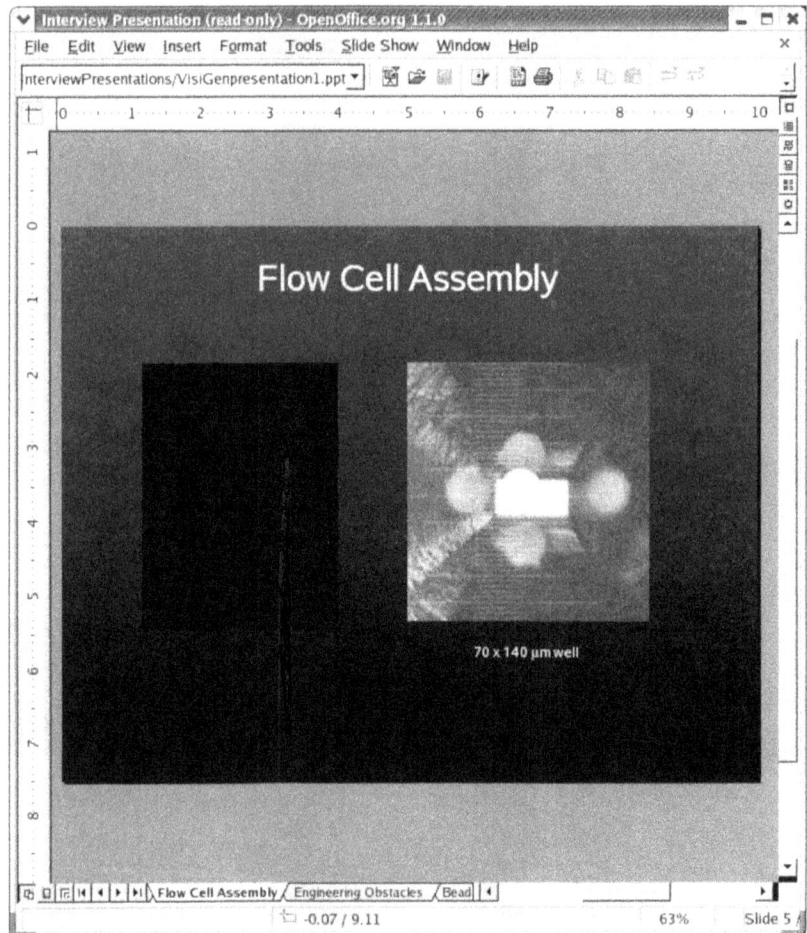

eSQL, plus many others. The MDB Tools package can be found at http://mdbtools.sourceforge.net, and can be built as follows:

```
# tar -tzf mdbtools-0.5.tar.gz
# cd mdbtools-0.5
# ./configure
# make
# make install
Now to list all those commands that come with this package:
# mdb-<tab>
mdb-array     mdb-export     mdb-parsecsv   mdb-sql      mdb-ver
mdb-dump      mdb-header     mdb-schema     mdb-tables
```

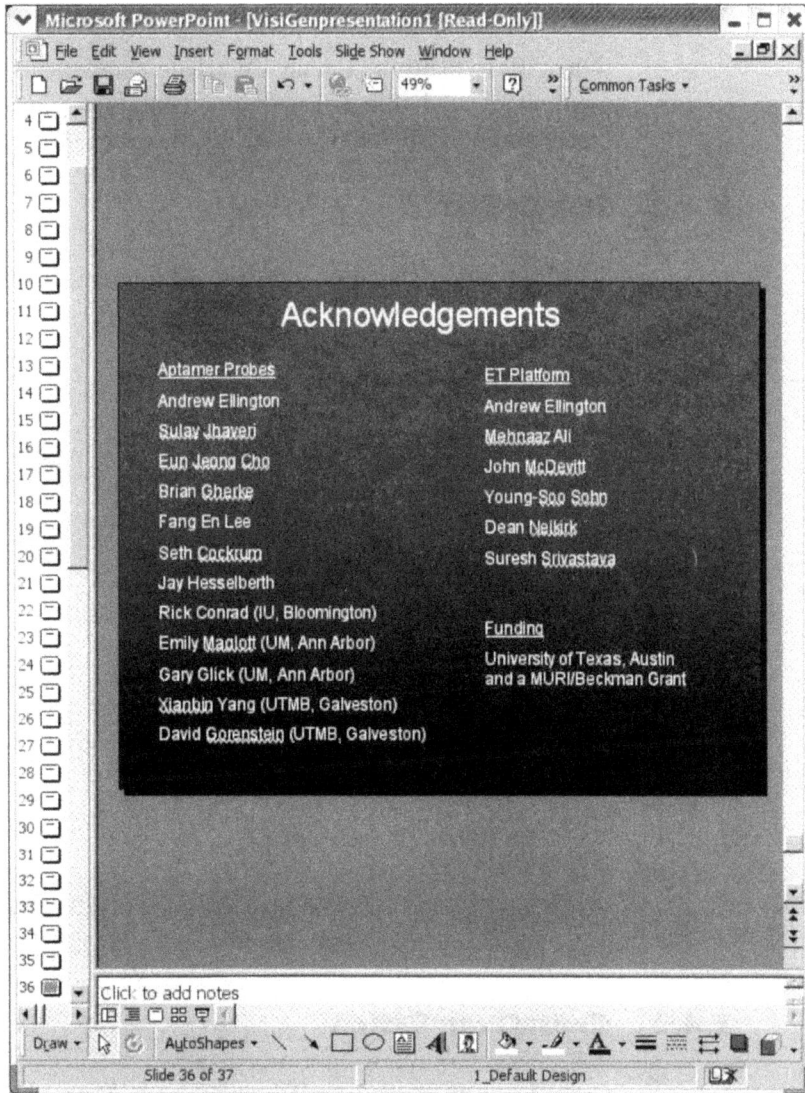

Figure 3.7
*Comparison of
Powerpoint Text
Layout.*

The gmdb2 GUI program can be used in a similar form to Access, but it has no ability to write to the database file yet, however it provides a graphical interface for the export of the Access database into files readable by the more powerful MySQL or PostgreSQL programs. Version 0.6 is supposed to have write access, but it is still in beta. Here is the view of access using CrossOver Office (see Figure 3.8), while Figure 3.9 displays a similar scene using gmbd2 interface. While similar the gmdb2 interface is read only.

So let's look once more at our trio of solutions.

3.4.1   OpenOffice

OpenOffice does not contain a database component. There are, however, methods to read this data within OpenOffice; since these methods are based on the MDB Tools package, there is no read/write capability.

3.4.2   StarOffice

StarOffice does contain a database component, but it is ADABAS, not Access.

Figure 3.8
Access.

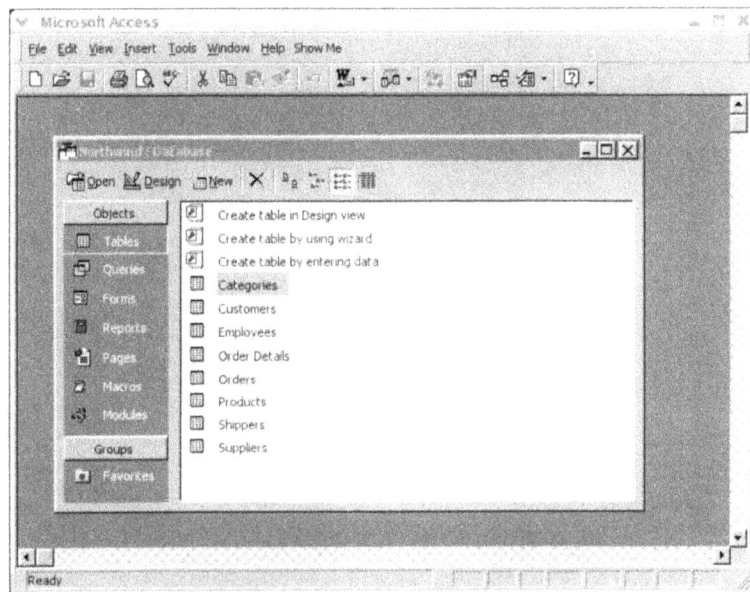

3.4.3   CrossOver Office

CrossOver Office emulates Windows using Wine. Since it does, all Access capability is available to the user; however, you should be concerned about the more esoteric functions and plug-ins, since they may not work within this emulation environment.

3.5   FrontPage-Produced Web Pages

The subject of editing Web pages and configuring your Web browser is covered in Chapter 4.

Figure 3.9
MDBTools.

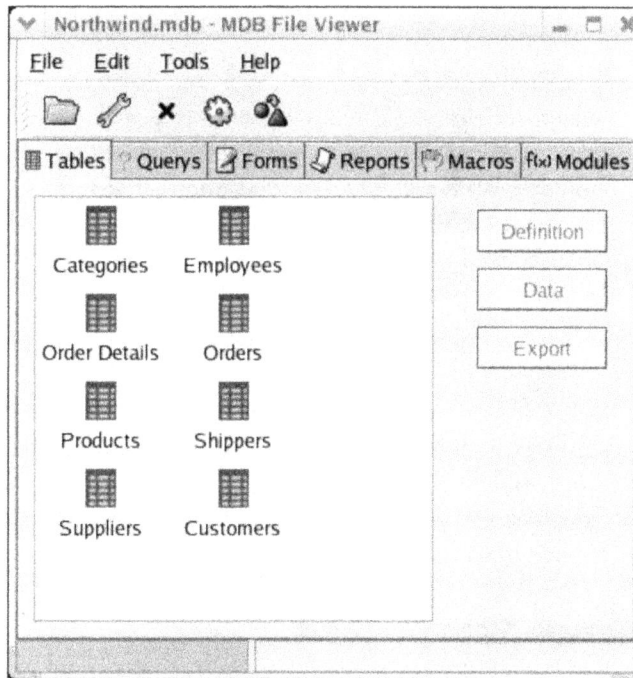

3.6   Visio

Unfortunately, Linux does not have a native Visio document tool; however, it does boast tools that are similar to Visio, including Kivio, DIA (www.gnome.org/projects/dia/), and xfig. Kivio, a part of Koffice, provides a Visio look and feel, while DIA provides a standard drawing canvas that has stencil support. Yet neither can read Visio documents, since the files have a proprietary format. Various groups are trying to decode this, but no program can truly replace Visio. So what options really exist?

3.6.1   CrossOver Office

The CrossOver Office emulation environment, which is an enhanced version of Wine, will allow you to run Visio locally on your Linux desktop. Since this is an emulation, there may be issues with any sort of plug-ins.

3.7   **WordPerfect**

WordPerfect (WP8) for Linux will read and write WordPerfect and many versions of Microsoft Word documents as well. This is another alternative to using OpenOffice or CrossOver office for editing Word documents. However, WP8 is an older product and therefore does not understand modern Microsoft Word file formats. WP8 for Linux is no longer available from Corel, so we have to make do with secondary locations. A version of WP8 for Linux is available at www.linuxmafia.com/wpfaq.

WP8 is not valid for a commercial setting, and requires a much older version of the Linux system to work. In essence, you want to look at the CLOS Deluxe Edition v 1.2 boxed set editions. Once again, because it's not modern, WP8 for Linux may not work on recent Linux operating systems, and it is incredibly hard to find. While you can install WP8 using libraries from the older systems placed in a separate directory structure it is a non-trivial method to gain this support, Appendix C contains the details.

3.8   **Exchange Server Mail**

Exchange Server Mail can be accessed by a number of means, either using the Exchange Server Mail protocols or using IMAP.

The easiest to use is Exchange via your Web browser. This has the advantage of not needing any special setup except on your Exchange Server itself. Any Web browser can access this mechanism, and you can access as many mailboxes as necessary via the Web interface. The most commonly used Web browser on Linux is Mozilla. No special plug-ins are necessary to use Exchange in this fashion, just the necessary setup for your Exchange server. This will give you full access to your mailbox, including all folders; remember, though, that e-mail takes up a *lot* of desktop space. Using a link similar to the following will access your e-mail if the OWA service of Exchange is enabled:

`http://servername/exchange/e-mail.address`
Where `servername` is the name of your exchange server, and `e-mail.address` is your mail address.

Alternatively, you can access your e-mail via IMAP. IMAP access limits your access to just your Exchange e-mail, such that your calendar and other folders are *not* available via IMAP. Popular e-mail clients that can handle IMAP include MozillaMail, Evolution, Thunderbird, MUTT, PINE, ELM, as well as many other mail clients not part of modern Linux distributions. To configure, specify that you will use IMAP and the IP address or Exchange servername where appropriate. For outgoing e-mail you may use your Exchange server again, or there may be an SMTP server somewhere else.

There are two special-case clients, however, that allow you to access your full mailbox via Exchange. The first, Ximian Evolution Connector, depends on Ximian Evolution. The Connector will access Exchange as if it were an Outlook-style client, and gain access to all your folders, including a global address list, and your calendar. Unfortunately, it cannot easily access your group or public folders, or even add another mailbox that you could normally access in Exchange. Setting up Ximian Evolution Connector can be a little daunting, so here are the steps you should take:

3.8.1 Red Hat Enterprise Linux Version 3 (RHEL3)

1. Run *up2date –nox –i evolution-connector*, since Evolution is available as a part of the default installation.

   Now that Evolution and the Connector are installed, you can add an account using the Evolution account creator. When you first start Evolution, you will receive the screen shown in Figure 3.10. You should then click on forward.

2. You will proceed through the appropriate screens, entering the appropriate content, until you reach the screen displayed in Figure 3.11, where you will select Microsoft Exchange from the menu.

3. You will be asked then enter in the information about your Exchange server, including your Windows Username, as shown in Figure 3.12. This username can include your Windows Domain and Username in the format of DOMAIN\Username. Please note that the backslash (\) is very important; it is not a forward slash (/).

4. Next, you will be asked to enter your Global Catalog Server Name used for a Global Address List, as shown in Figure 3.13. This information is readily available from your Exchange Admins.

5. Once the configuration is completed, you will then have to restart Evolution for the changes to Connector to take effect. Enable Folder view, and your Exchange Account will be visible. Expanding this account will ask you for your password, which you then enter to access Exchange Mail via Evolution Connector.

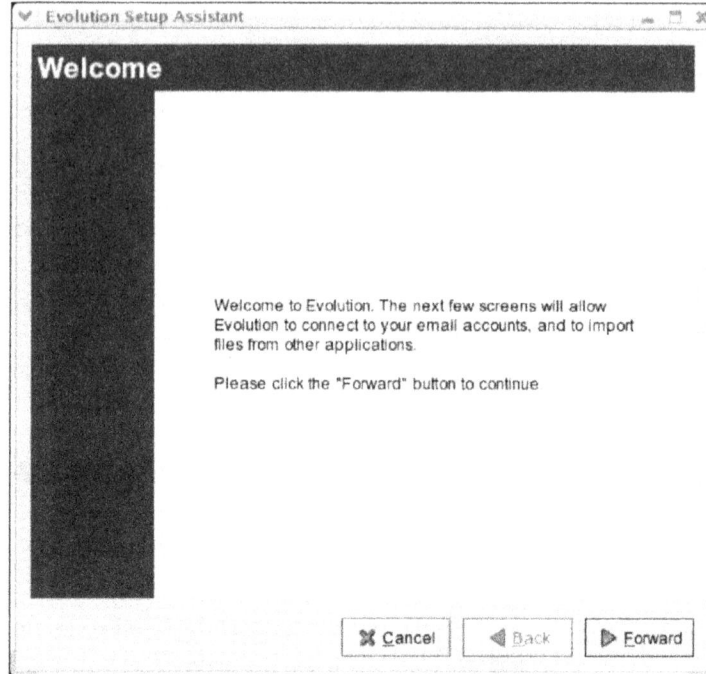

Welcome to Evolution. The next few screens will allow Evolution to connect to your email accounts, and to import files from other applications.

Please click the "Forward" button to continue

Please enter information about your incoming mail server below. If you are not sure, ask your system administrator or Internet Service Provider.

Server Type: None

Description:

Figure 3.12
*Evolution setup
assistant: receiving
mail (Exchange).*

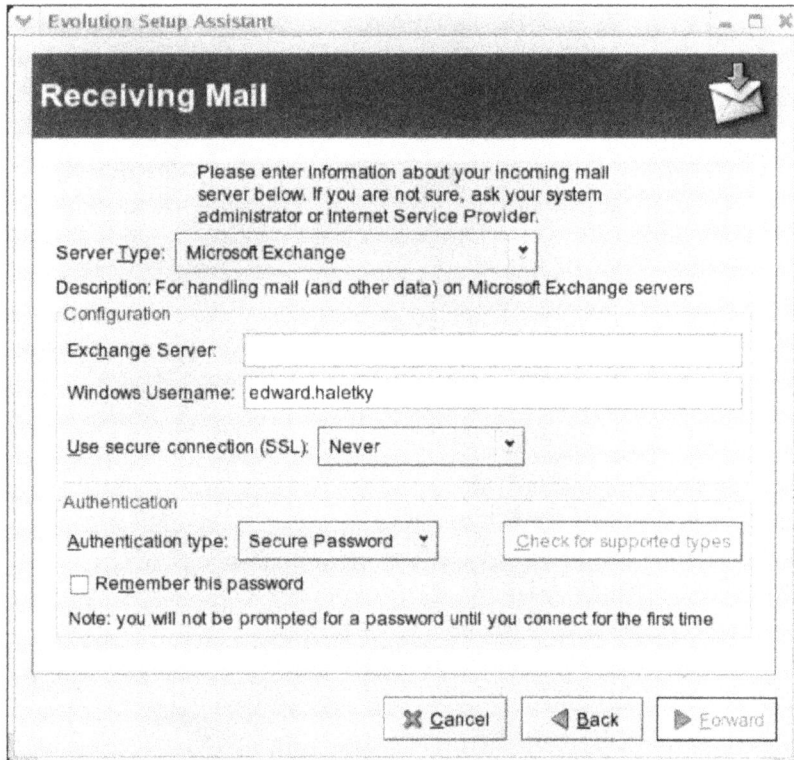

All this talk about Evolution startup, and nothing about older e-mail? If you want all your archived or current local e-mail that is saved in a .PST file created by Microsoft Outlook, you will have to migrate it across. To pull all this information from your .PST to your Evolution mailbox, you will need to follow these steps:

1. Install Mozilla for Windows on a Windows machine.

2. Verify that any foldername with a / in it has been renamed inside Exchange.

3. Import your PST and PAB files into Mozilla.

4. Copy the resultant .slt directory to Linux.

5. Run the *mozillatoevo.sh* (see the following code) to import the complete .slt directory into Evolution. Please make sure Evolution is not running when you do this.

Figure 3.13
*Evolution setup
assistant: receiving
mail (Global
Address List).*

```
mozillatoevo.sh
#!/bin/bash

function fmetadata {
echo '<?xml version="1.0"?>' > "$evodir/folder-metadata.xml"
echo '<efolder>' >> "$evodir/folder-metadata.xml"
echo '<type>mail</type>' >> "$evodir/folder-metadata.xml"
echo '<description></description>' >> "$evodir/folder-
metadata.xml"
echo '</efolder>' >> "$evodir/folder-metadata.xml"
}

function lmetadata {
echo '<?xml version="1.0"?>' > "$evodir/local-metadata.xml"
echo '<folderinfo>' >> "$evodir/local-metadata.xml"
echo '<folder type="mbox" name="mbox" index="1"/>' >> "$evodir/
local-metadata.xml"
echo '</folderinfo>' >> "$evodir/local-metadata.xml"
}
```

```
function localmail {
    # now handle non-folders
    cd "$mozdir"
    foo=`ls | awk '$0 !~ /\./ {printf "%s",$0}'`
    IFS=''
    for y in $foo
    do
        if [ -f "$y" ]
        then
            echo "Working on $y"
            oevodir="$evodir"
            evodir="$evodir/$y"
            mkdir -p "$evodir"
            cp "$y" "$evodir"/mbox
            fmetadata
            lmetadata
            if [ -d "$y.sbd" ]
            then
                evodir="$evodir/subfolders"
                mozdir="$mozdir/$y.sbd"
                localmail
                mozdir=`dirname "$mozdir"`
                evodir=`dirname "$evodir"`
                cd $mozdir
            fi
            evodir=`dirname "$evodir"`
        fi
    done
}

MozillaDir=$1
echo "Tool to convert Mozilla mail to Evolution"
echo "Tool to convert Outlook mail converted to Mozilla to
Evolution"

if [ -d "$MozillaDir" ]
then
    cd "$MozillaDir"
else
    echo "Please enter a valid Mozilla .sbd directory."
    echo "I.e. mozillatoevo.sh ~/.mozilla/default/
Op4nbns6z.slt/Mail/Local Folder/Outlook Mail.sbd"
    exit
fi

mozdir="$MozillaDir"
evodir="$HOME/evolution/local"
```

```
cd "$mozdir"
localmail
```

Now you have a mail client that can be used to access Exchange, including calendar and other features of the standard Exchange client. However, it still has its limitations. You will not be able to access group mailboxes, and if these are needed, you may have to pursue this with other tools.

In the beginning, we mentioned a second special case, that is, using CrossOver Office to run Microsoft Outlook emulated by Wine. In this way, you can have full access via a standard Outlook client. It should be noted that many plug-ins for Outlook will not work, nor will the esoteric features, since the underlying layer does not yet have the capability to handle these. However, group and normal mailbox access do work as well as the standard Outlook views.

3.9   Printing (Network or Attached)

Printing to a generic network printer requires knowing two things for Linux. First, you need to know the IP address of the device, and second, you need to know the type of device to use. For a generic attached printer, only the device type is required; then it is just a case of setting up the printer and picking the proper printing options. As with everything in Linux, there is more than one way to do this, but the easiest by far is to use one of the GUI tools to set up your printer. However, which tool to use depends on the printer subsystem to be used. Most Linux systems today use the CUPS printer subsystem, rather than the older Berkeley subsystem. Use of the configuration tools is covered in depth outside this book.

RHEL3: redhat-config-printer
Mandrake: drakconf
SuSE: yast2
Fedora/RHEL4: system-config-printer

3.9.1   Printing to a Windows print server

Printing to a Windows print server is quite simple to do and can be performed using either the Berkeley or CUPS printer subsystem. The major caveat for accessing a Windows print server is authentication. If the server requires authentication, as is the case for most printers, you will need to either hardcode a password into the Linux configuration for the printer or use a command-line tool such as smbclient, where you enter the password at print time or use a credentials file.

3.9.2   **Printing to an AppleTalk or Macintosh printer**

Modern Macintosh computers are very easy to configure to use any printer, since they use many of the same tools available to Linux. You can set up your Mac to act as a CIFS server and use Windows-style authentication, as described previously. Or you can use a UNIX-like printer daemon running on the Mac, which will manage the entire Mac, as well as attached or AppleTalk printers.

Note: Access to older Macs require the netatalk package as does access to any Macintosh Ethertalk network attached printer. Netatalk setup is beyond the scope of this book.

3.10   **Other Considerations**

There are also other issues to consider when using Linux-based tools to replace Office products. As we stated previously, several formatting issues arise when using the OpenOffice and StarOffice word processing programs. One way to alleviate these issues is to use different fonts, since many of the fonts available on Microsoft (e.g., Arial) are not available on Linux. An open-source project exists (http://corefonts.sourceforge.net) to solve this problem. Another solution is to use an existing set of fonts available from the C:\Windows\Fonts directory on a Windows box. To use either of these solutions to help with formatting issues, use the following recipe for each of the corefonts mentioned.

```
# rpmbuild --rebuild cabextract-0.6-1.src.rpm
Installing cabextract-0.6-1.src.rpm
...
Wrote: /usr/src/redhat/RPMS/i386/cabextract-0.6-1.i386.rpm
...
# rpm -ivh /usr/sec/redhat/RPMS/i386/cabextract-0.6-
1.i386..rpm
# cabextract arial32.exe
Extracting cabinet: arial32.exe
  extracting: FONTINST.EXE
  extracting: fontinst.inf
  extracting: Ariali.TTF
```

```
    extracting: Arialbd.TTF
    extracting: Arialbi.TTF
    extracting: Arial.TTF
Finished processing cabinet.
# cabextract andale32.exe
Extracting cabinet: andale32.exe
    extracting: fontinst.inf
    extracting: andale.inf
    extracting: fontinst.exe
    extracting: AndaleMo.TTF
    extracting: ADVPACK.DLL
    extracting: W95INF32.DLL
    extracting: W95INF16.DLL
Finished processing cabinet.
Perform for each font downloaded.
# mkdir /usr/share/fonts/ttf
# cp *.TTF /usr/share/fonts/ttf
* or * copy from a Windows Font directory
# cd /usr/share/fonts/ttf
# ttmkfdir
# mkfontdir
# chkfontpath -a /usr/share/fonts/ttf

Now set default text font in OpenOffice to Arial
```

Using Microsoft fonts will aid in solving some of your formatting issues, but not all of them.

3.11   Easy Answer

There is an easy answer to solving your Office program issues on Linux, and that is to use VMware to run a Virtual Machine session in a Window on your desktop. This gives you a complete Windows environment in which you can use your common desktop tools without depending on Linux tools. However, VMware is an expensive option, at $199 per seat plus a license for Windows.

3.12   The Cost

Is there a cost to using Linux to replace your Office tools? In a nutshell, there is, either in functionality or in price. As you get closer and closer to achieving the full functionality of Microsoft Office, your expenditures will go up, since you are then looking at the "easy answer" for the desktop.

However, if you do not need all the formatting bells and whistles, then CrossOver Office may work for you. While it does have its problems with plug-ins, CrossOver Office will get the job done. Lastly, if you are unconcerned about final editing, or are using a homogenous Linux environment, you can use the OpenOffice or StarOffice tools.

One of the most widely used tools on any system is e-mail, and multiple methods exist for accessing your e-mail, as discussed previously. The most widely used are Evolution with the now free Exchange Connector, or OWA via the Web.

Potential costs for Linux replacements for Office tools are displayed in Table 3.1.

Table 3.1   *Cost of Linux Replacements for Office Tools*

Software	Support Level	Fee	Support Fee
OpenOffice	OpenSource	NA	NA
StarOffice	Web-based/Phone	$80	Free for 60 days
VMware	Web-based/Phone	$199	Free for 90 days
Evolution w/Connector	OpenSource	NA	NA
Mozilla	OpenSource	NA	NA
CrossOver Office	Web Based	$60	Free for 90 days

4

Multimedia, Web Browsing, and Publishing

Probably the most important tool for any desktop user is the Web browser. While Mozilla (or Firefox) is the browser of choice for Linux, it is not as complete as Internet Explorer out of the box. We will document ways to enhance Mozilla to come up to par with Internet Explorer. As in the previous chapter, we will discuss standalone Linux, Wine, and the use of VMware to provide solutions to the sticky problem of making Mozilla behave in as integrated a manner with the Linux desktop as Internet Explorer does with Microsoft Windows.

4.1   **Plug-ins**

There are many plug-ins available for the native Linux browser, Mozilla. Some of these plug-ins are pure plug-ins designed specifically for Mozilla; others invoke system tools to display the Web content. We will split the plug-ins between the pure and the invoked. However, the display of multimedia content is included under the pure plug-ins. This audio and video content has both pure and invoked plug-ins and is a section unto itself. The best location for Mozilla plug-in information is at http://plugin-doc.mozdev.org/linux.html, the Mozilla plug-in Web site for Linux. In this chapter, we will discuss what is required to install the plug-ins.

If a plug-in does not appear, or is duplicated by another plug-in, you may need to remove the file *.mozilla/pluginreg.dat* to effect the change to the plug-ins you desire. Removal of this file will not affect your plug-ins, except to force reregistration.

4.1.1   How Do I View Java Web Content?

First you will need at least version 1.4.2 of Java Runtime Environment (JRE) installed on your system. In most cases, JRE is not available off the installation media, so you will need to download this from the Java Web site.

RHEL3

The Java implementation that ships with RHEL3 is the Java of choice. Install the IBM Java package in Red Hat Package Manager (RPM) format from the Extras CD or Disk 9 (IBM Java2-JRE-1.4.1-8.i386.rpm). On install, this can also be done when the machine boots for the first time by selecting Extras.

```
# mount —o ro /dev/cdrom /mnt/cdrom
# cd /mnt/cdrom/RedHat/RPMS
# rpm —ivh IBMJava2-JRE-1.4.1-8.i386.rpm
```

Other versions

Download the RPM form of the J2RE from http://www.java.com/en/download/manual.jsp. Please note that the name of the file may change as newer versions of J2RE become available.

```
# ./j2re-1_4_1_02-linux-i586-rpm.bin
...
9. Termination   for   Infringement.   Either   party   may
terminate  this  Agreement  immediately  should any Software
become, or in either  party's  opinion  be likely to become,
the subject of a claim of infringement  of any  intellectual
property right.

For inquiries please contact:  Sun Microsystems,  Inc., 4150
Network  Circle,  Santa  Clara,  California   95054,  U.S.A.
(LFI#120080/Form ID#011801)


Do you agree to the above license terms? [yes or no]
yes
Unpacking...
Checksumming...
0
0
Extracting...
UnZipSFX 5.40 of 28 November 1998, by Info-ZIP (Zip-
Bugs@lists.wku.edu).
```

```
   inflating: j2re-1_4_1_02-fcs-linux-i586.rpm
Done.
# rpm —ivh j2re-1_4_1_02-fcs-linux-i586.rpm
```

Once the JRE is installed, using one of the previous methods, you are ready to hook Java into the Mozilla browser on your system. There are a few considerations at this point, pertaining to how your version of Mozilla was built. If your version of Mozilla was built using gcc3, as is the case with RHEL3, then your instructions differ slightly from those not built with gcc3.

Configuring the JRE plug-in

RHEL3

```
# ln -s /opt/IBMJava2-141/jre/bin/libjavaplugin_ojigcc3.so \
/usr/lib/mozilla/plugins/
```

SUN J2RE

```
# ln —s /usr/java/j2re1.4.1_02/plugin/i386/ns610/
libjavaplugin_oji.so \
/usr/lib/mozilla/plugins/
```

Configuring Java system-wide

Add a file to */etc/profile.d* named *java.sh* to add Java to the default *PATH*, using the appropriate *PATH* per the option installed. The contents of the file are:

```
if ! echo ${PATH} | grep -q /opt/IBMJava2-141/bin ; then
     PATH=/opt/IBMJava2-141/bin:${PATH}
fi
```

It should be noted that if you do not use a symbolic link and, instead, just copy the file, the Java plug-in will cease to function and could also cause your browser to inexplicably die. The symbolic link ensures that the JRE knows where to find all the Java functionality for your programs.

A good way to check whether Java works is to use the Mozilla menu option *Help->About Plug-ins* to display all the plug-ins currently available to your browser. If Java does not appear as shown in Figure 4.1, then there is a problem: either the permissions on the file are incorrect, you failed to use the proper file (i.e., a non-gcc3 version on a Mozilla built with gcc3), or the plug-in directory is not seen by Mozilla. Please note that we have docu-

Figure 4.1
*Mozilla plug-ins:
Java.*

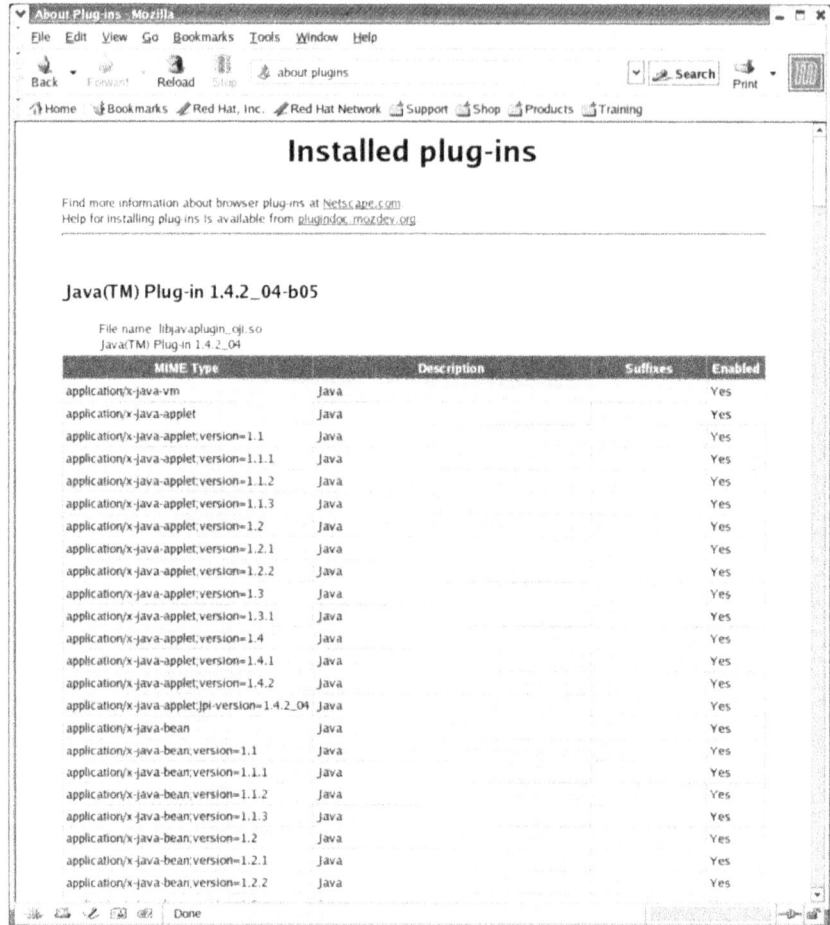

mented how to set up Java as a plug-in using the standard Mozilla that ships as a part of your operating system. Versions of Mozilla downloaded from http://www.mozilla.org may not install in the same directory, and will use a different plug-in directory or directories. After you are sure Mozilla sees that Java is installed, you will want to test your Java installation by pointing your browser to http://www.java.com/en/download/help/testvm.jsp, which tests your Java Virtual Machine and thereby your Java installation. Please note that you may have to reload the page to run the test.

How do I view Macromedia Flash Web content?

You will need the Macromedia Flash Linux plug-in from http://macromedia.com/shockwave/download/alternates. Download the Linux x86 with the (2) beside it, since this is a supported RPM version. Installation of this

Figure 4.2

*Mozilla plug-ins:
Macromedia Flash.*

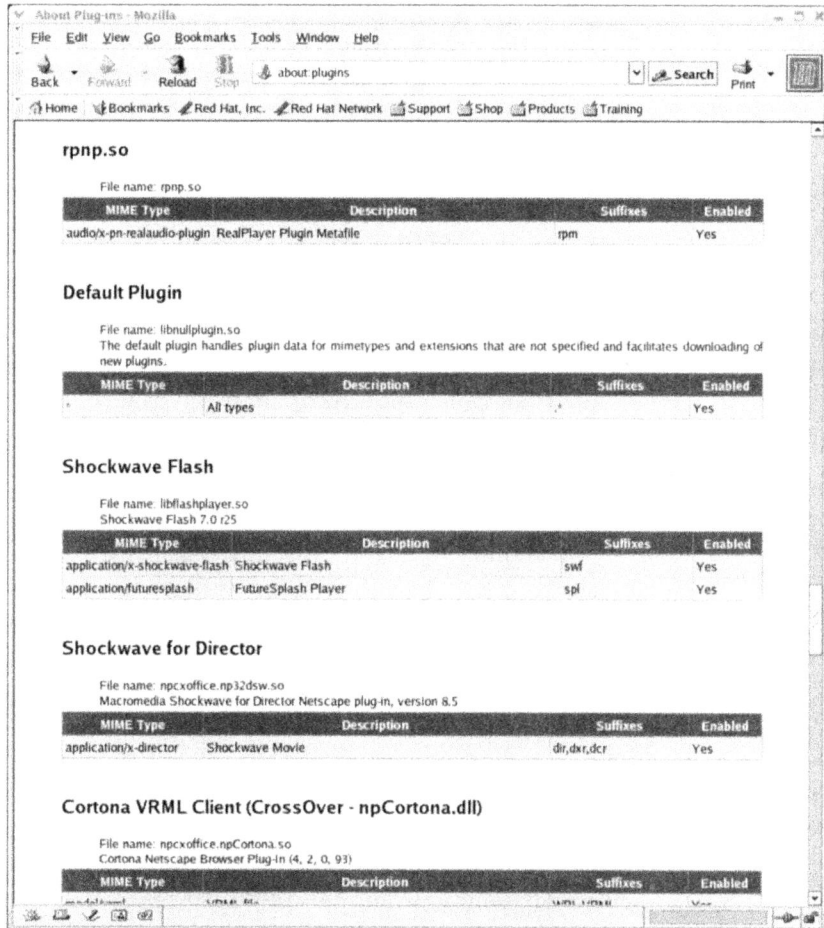

Figure 4.2

Mozilla plug-ins: Macromedia Flash.

RPM is the same for every form of Linux that uses RPM, with the exception that a pop-up window appears with the license agreement, which you must "Accept" to continue. The plug-in installation will also find the current version of Mozilla on your system and place the files in the appropriate directory.

RHEL3

Download the *flash-plugin-6.0.81-1.RHEL.i386.rpm* from the Red Hat Network, and then install this RPM. This RPM is usually behind, so you may wish to follow the steps for Other (below) to install the most recent plug-in, but be sure to remove the RPM plug-in if necessary.

```
up2date flash-plugin
```

Other

```
% rpm -ivh flash-plugin-6.0.79-2.i386.rpm
# Accept the popup window license agreement
Registering flashplayer as a XPCOM component in
/usr/lib/mozilla-1.4
Setup is complete.
```

After the RPM is installed, verify that Mozilla has loaded it by using the Mozilla menu option *Help->About Plug-ins* to display all the plug-ins currently available to your browser.

If Flash does not appear as shown in Figure 4.2, then you experienced an installation issue, most likely caused by your browser not recognizing the plug-in directory into which the plug-in was installed. Please note that these instructions are for the standard installation of Mozilla that comes with your Linux release, not a downloaded copy of Mozilla.

In addition, you can verify that Flash is working correctly by pointing your browser to http://www.macromedia.com/, since the main site for Macromedia uses Flash at the top of the page to display its own advertisements.

4.1.2   How Do I View Adobe Acrobat Web content?

There are two viewers for Adobe Acrobat Web content with Mozilla. One is to use the Xpdf viewer that ships as a part of many Linux distributions; the other is to use the Linux version of the official Adobe Acrobat Reader. This viewer, available from Adobe (ftp://download.adobe.com/pub/adobe/acrobatreader/unix/), is not normally a part of a Linux distribution. Using one over the other depends on which newer features of PDF documents you will be using, since Xpdf, as with most open-source products, lags behind the code developed by software makers. Since both viewers are free of charge and the viewer from Adobe is integrated into Mozilla via the programmatic plug-in interface, it may be a cleaner solution.

To use Xpdf as a viewer, refer to section 4.1.7.

To install Adobe Acrobat viewer:

RHEL3

```
# up2date acroread acroread-plugin

# mkdir acrobat
# cd acrobat
```

```
# tar -xzf ../linux-508.tar.gz
# INSTALL

ADOBE SYSTEMS INCORPORATED

...

Please type "accept" to accept the terms and conditions license
agreement; Type "decline" to exit. accept

This installation requires 25MB of free disk space.

Enter installation directory for Acrobat 5.0.8 [/usr/local/
Acrobat5]

Directory "/usr/local/Acrobat5" does not exist.
Do you want to create it now? [y]

Installing platform independent files ... Done

Installing platform dependent files ... Done

# cd ..
# rm -rf acrobat
# ln -s /usr/local/Acrobat5/Browsers/intellinux/nppdf.so /usr/
lib/mozilla/plugins
# chmod 755 /usr/lib/mozilla/plugins/nppdf.so
# ln -s /usr/local/Acrobat5/bin/acroread /usr/local/bin/
acroread
```

If you are using Red Hat 8.0 or later, edit */usr/local/Acrobat5/bin/acroread* as root, and add the following below the first two lines of the file:

```
LANG=en_US
export LANG
```

If you are using Mandrake 9.x, edit */usr/local/Acrobat5/bin/acroread* as root, and add the following below the first two lines of the file:

```
LC_CTYPE=C
export LC_CTYPE
```

It should be noted that while you can use both of these to view Web content, you can also use them to view locally stored PDF content. Many

Figure 4.3
*Mozilla plug-ins:
PDF.*

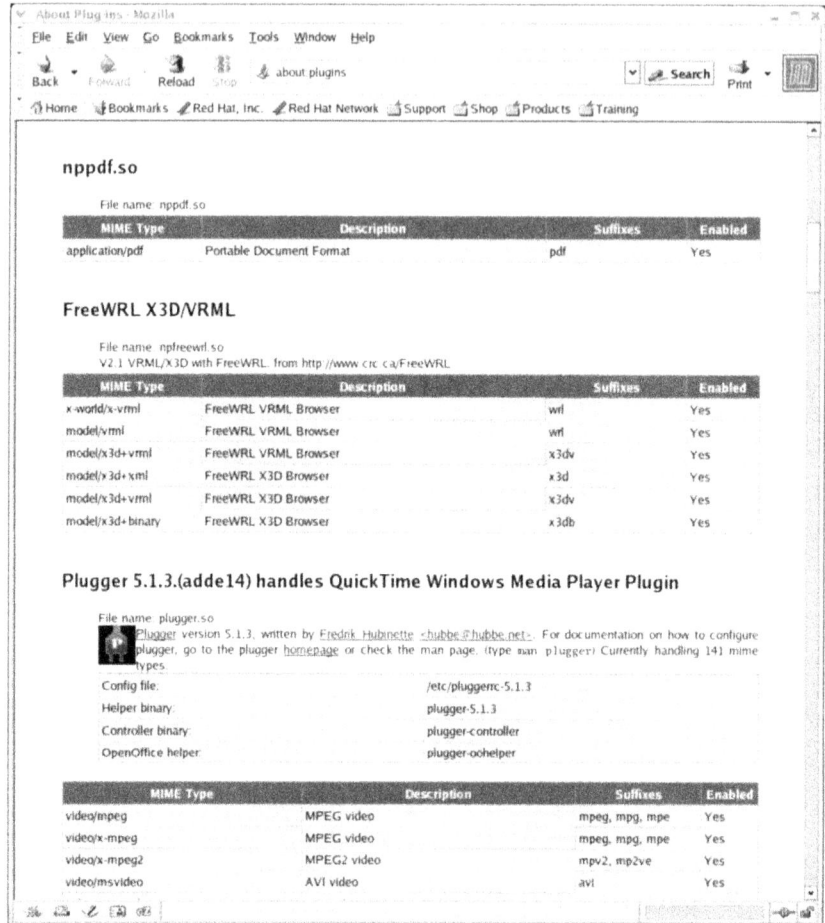

of the desktop tools will integrate into their folder viewers' access to one if not both of these tools or provide methods to add one of these as default viewers. Last, you can always use the *acroread* command from the command line.

Point your browser to www.adobe.com/products/acrobat/pdfs/pdfarchiving.pdf to test your PDF configuration after you verify when you go to *Help->About Plug-ins* in the Mozilla browser shows the `nppdf.so` plugin available, as displayed in Figure 4.3.

How do I add Adobe Acrobat to GNOME?

From where you download your RPMs for Acrobat will determine whether there exists the automated method for adding Acrobat to GNOME. There are two parts to this integration: the first is to add Acrobat to the menu subsystem, and the second is to make it a viewer for the *nautilus* folder viewer and browser. If you install the RPM direct from RedHat these steps can be ignored.

Adding to menus

```
# cd /usr/share/applications
# cp net-Xpdf.desktop net-acroread.desktop
Edit net-acroread.desktop and change the Name= and Exec= lines
to read:
     Name=Adobe Acrobat
     Exec=acroread
Then save the file
```

Adding to Nautilus

As long as *acroread* is in your path, Nautilus can use it to open local PDF content. However, you will need to edit your file types (*Red Fedora -> Preferences -> File Types and Programs*) to make it the default viewer.

How do I add Adobe Acrobat to KDE?

As with integrating into GNOME, integration into the K Desktop Environment (KDE) requires a two-phase setup into the KDE menuing system and its *Konqueror* folder viewer and browser. If installed from the Red Hat Network via up2date the following steps can be ignored, but its always good to verify all is properly configured.

Adding to menus

Right-click on the *Red Fedora->Menu Editor*, select Documentation on the left side menu, and press *New Item*. When the *New Item* menu appears, enter *Acrobat* and press *OK*. The *Acrobat* entry will appear under *Documentation* on the left side, and on the right will be the entry for the command to use with this menu item. In the entry box for *Command*, enter */usr/local/bin/acroread*, then click on *Apply*, and select *File->Quit*. Before you select *File->Quit*, the Edit K Menu window should look like Figure 4.4.

Adding to Konqueror

To add Adobe Acrobat to Konqueror, first launch Konqueror by using *Red Fedora (start)->Home* menu option. Next, from within Konqueror use *Tools->Configure Konqueror* to launch the Settings window, and select *File Associations* from the left window. In the middle Known Types window, expand *application* and select *pdf*. Once you have that completed, press the *Add...* button and in the first entry box type in */usr/local/bin/acroread* and click *OK*.

Figure 4.4
*The Edit K menu
for adding Acrobat.*

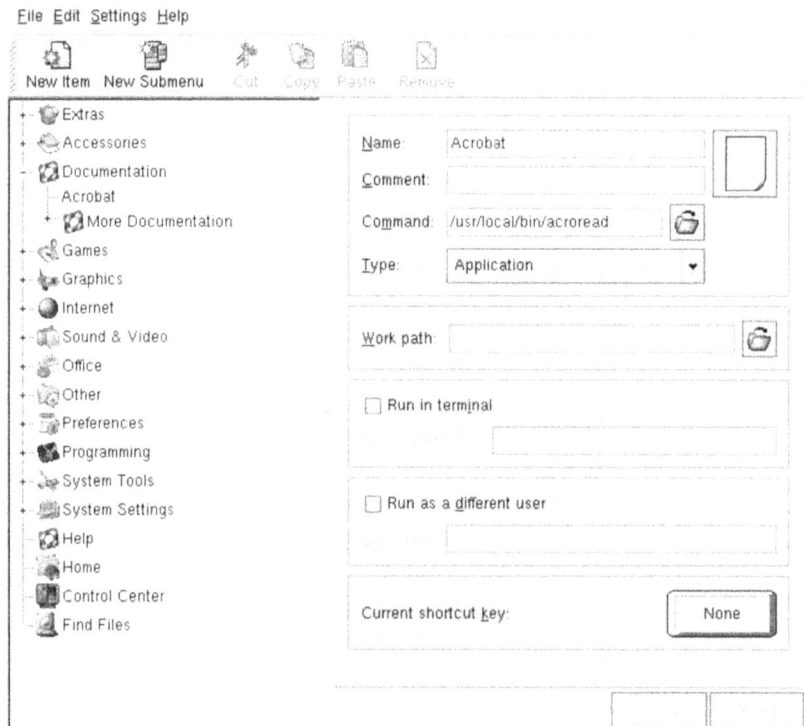

Finally, select *acroread* and, using the *Move Up* button, move *acroread* to the top of the list before clicking *Apply* and then *OK* to exit the Settings window. Your window before pressing *Apply* should look like Figure 4.5.

How do I add Adobe Acrobat into Evolution?

As long as *acroread* is in your *PATH*, Evolution can use this program to open and view PDF documents. If the viewer is not in your *PATH*, the *Open in Adobe Acrobat...* viewer option will not appear.

4.1.3   How Do I View VRML Web content?

Virtual Reality Modeling Language (VRML) is used to display 3D graphic objects within a Web browser. Unlike the other plug-ins, this one installs very differently and has some specific requirements to work; it is not a straightforward installation of a prebuilt RPM or package, but the compilation of a plug-in from source. To view VRML content:

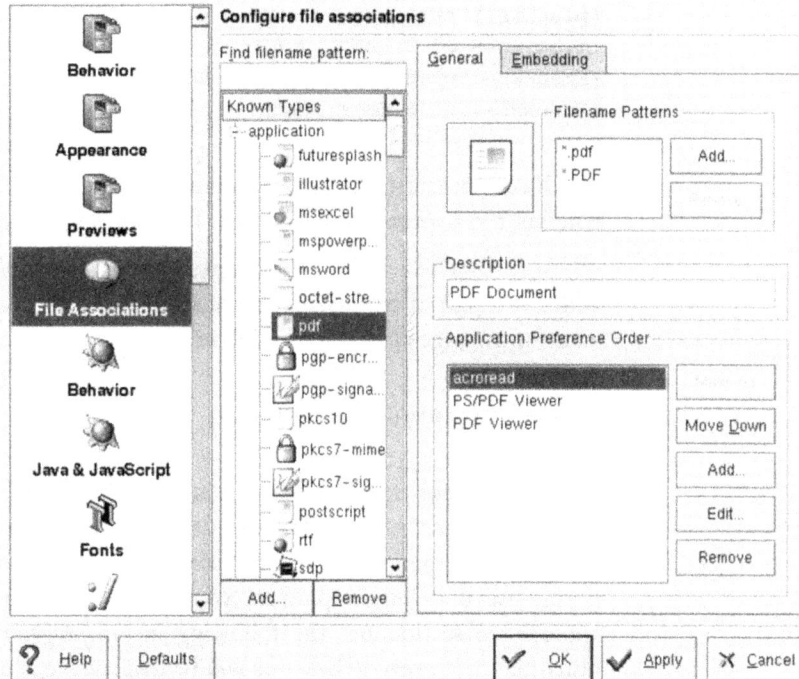

Figure 4.5
*Adding Adobe
Acrobat: the
Settings window
for Konqueror.*

- Java must be installed, and the Java bin directory must be in your *PATH* (if you install the JRE and JDK that are part of the releases mentioned previously, you will have everything you need).

- gcc must be installed.

- Perl must be installed.

- The basic Linux development environment must be installed.

While gcc, Perl, and the development environments are available from your operating system CD-ROMs, Java should be installed as described previously or as your Java distribution describes. In the following build script, we have used IBM Java, which is provided on the RHEL3.0 CD-ROM. However, any Java will work, and the *PATH* setting needs to be modified accordingly.

Building VRML

```
Script started on Sat 24 Apr 2004 11:18:00 AM EDT
[plugins]$ PATH=/opt/IBMJava2-141/bin:${PATH}
[plugins]$ export PATH
```

```
[plugins]$ ln
[plugins]$ tar -xzf FreeWRL-1.03.tar.gz
[plugins]$ cd FreeWRL-1.03
[FreeWRL-1.03]$ perl Makefile.PL
[FreeWRL-1.03]$ make install
```

Once again, use the Mozilla menu *Help->About Plug-ins* to determine whether the *npfreewrl.so* plug-in has been loaded, as shown in Figure 4.3.

To further test this functionality, issue the *freewrl* command that was added as a part of the installation procedure. A box may appear briefly with an error message similar to the following:

```
FreeWRL Exiting — File was not found.
```

This message at least tells us that the display driver has everything it needs; otherwise, you would see a *No visual found* error. A good site to view as a test would be *file:///home/user/FreeWRL-1.03/tests/collision.wrl*. However, if you use the Plugger plug-in, you will also have to comment out the appropriate section per the following in */etc/pluggerrc-5.0*. It should be noted that not every VRML file will be displayable, since there are multiple versions of VRML available.

```
##
## Virtual Reality Modeling Language - VRML
##
# model/vrml:vrl,vrml:Virtual Reality Modeling Language
# model/x-vrml:vrl:Virtual Reality Modeling Language
# world/vrml:vrl,vrml:Virtual Reality Modeling Language
# world/x-vrml:vrl:Virtual Reality Modeling Language
# x-world/vrml:vrl,vrml:Virtual Reality Modeling Language
# x-world/x-vrml:vrl:Virtual Reality Modeling Language
#       swallow(VRWeb Scene Viewer) fill: vrWeb -geometry
+9000+9000  -URL "$url" "$file" >/dev/null 2>/dev/null
```

4.1.4   How Do I View RealPlayer Streaming Media Web Content?

RealPlayer content can be viewed by installing the RealPlayer 8 RPM available from http://scopes.real.com/real/player/unix/unix.html, where you will have to enter some basic information before proceeding. Alternately, you can get RealPlayer from the Linux vendor. This is a fairly straightforward installation.

Figure 4.6
RealPlayer
graphical
configuration tool.

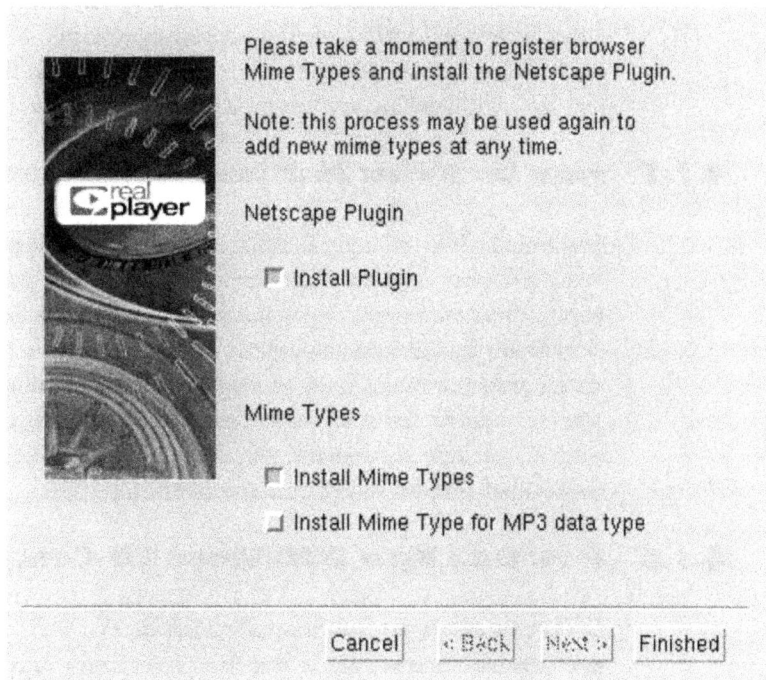

RHEL3

```
# up2date realplay
```

Other

```
ln —s /usr/lib/mozilla /usr/local/netscape
mv rp8_linux20_libc6_i386_cs2_rpm
rp8_linux20_libc6_i386_cs2.rpm
rpm —ivh rp8_linux20_libc6_i386_cs2.rpm
```

Once the RPM installs, you will be presented with a graphical configuration tool, as shown in Figure 4.6. I unselect installing for MP3 data type so that other programs can play the MP3 Content.

Press *Finished* and then *Next* > and finally *OK* to fully install the plug-in for Mozilla to use. Finally, after a small delay, you will be presented with the RealPlayer Configuration window for you to complete as you desire. During this phase, RealPlayer will connect to the Web and play back audio for you to hear and verify that the player is working. Once more, use the Mozilla menu *Help->About Plug-ins* to determine if the *rpnp.so* plug-in has been loaded.

To verify that RealPlayer is working, you can point your Web browser to http://www.npr.org/realmedia/programstream.ram. Since this is RealPlayer version 8, you many not be able to play all RealMedia content. Also, note that you will need an account to access much of the content.

4.1.5 How Do I View Multimedia Web Content?

Multimedia Web content is difficult to display as Web content, since it has many different formats. We therefore need to split this up by what are the most important items to view, since most of the tools listed here serve double duty as invoked programs that can be used to view or listen to stored multimedia presentations. While we cover the most popular options, we will also provide a matrix for many of the other esoteric types of audio or video content. All of these viewers and players require the Mozilla Plugger plug-in to be installed and, in some cases, specialized software.

4.1.6 How Do I View DVD/Video CD Content?

DVD content is not traditionally Multimedia Web content, but it is still multimedia content and is therefore a necessary topic to cover before we continue. To play a DVD, you must install a program that is the basis for viewing and playing most of the other multimedia formats. DVDs can be played using the *mplayer* program, downloaded from the www.mplayerhq.hu/homepage/ Web site and installed by using many RPM packages. Download all the packages into a newly created directory so that you can install them with a simple RPM command. There are a number of items you should download in several categories. You absolutely need the following RPMs:

mplayer-common

mplayer

mplayer-gui

Default skin package

Mplayer depends on the following minimal version packages, which are available as a part of your Operating System Media:

SDL-1.2.3-7

Xfree86-libs-4.2.0-8

audiofile-0.2.3-1

freetype-2.0.9-2

libjpeg-6b-19

libogg-1.0rc3-1

libpng-1.0.14-0.7x.3

libtermcap-2.0.8-28

libvorbis-1.0rc3-1

zlib-1.1.3-25.7

libgcc-3.2.2-5 (required for VIDIX support)

glib-1.2.10-5 (required for GUI support)

gtk+-1.2.10-15 (required for GUI support)

Also, you will need the following minimal version files from http://
ftp.icm.edu.pl/pub/linux/mplayer-rpms/apt/7.3/RPMS.testing/:

lame-3.95.1-1

lame-libs-3.95.1-1

lame-mp3x-3.95.1-1

Optionally, there are fonts and codecs that you can install as well.
Codecs are bits of code that will interpret the multimedia content for you.
The VIDIX codecs will only work on specific hardware; if that hardware
does not exist, VIDIX multimedia will NOT display.

Finally, you can also download an encoder.

The complete file list contains the following RPM packages.

Required packages:

mplayer-1.0pre3-1.i386.rpm

mplayer-common-1.0pre3-1.i386.rpm

mplayer-gui-1.0pre3-1.i386.rpm

mplayer-skin-default-1.0-2.noarch.rpm

Optional codecs:

mplayer-codecs-extralite-2.0-1.i386.rpm

mplayer-codecs-linux-real-9.0-1.i386.rpm

mplayer-codecs-linux-xanim-2.0-1.i386.rpm

mplayer-codecs-linux-xanim-3ivx-2.0-1.i386.rpm

mplayer-codecs-win32-2.0-1.i386.rpm

mplayer-codecs-win32-dmo-9.0-1.i386.rpm

mplayer-codecs-win32-indeo-2.0-1.i386.rpm

mplayer-codecs-win32-mjpeg2k-2.0-1.i386.rpm

mplayer-codecs-win32-qt-6.0-1.i386.rpm

mplayer-codecs-win32-qt-extras-2.0-1.i386.rpm

mplayer-vidix-1.0pre3-1.i386.rpm

mplayer-vidix-mach64-1.0pre3-1.i386.rpm

mplayer-vidix-mga-1.0pre3-1.i386.rpm

mplayer-vidix-nvidia-1.0pre3-1.i386.rpm

mplayer-vidix-permedia-1.0pre3-1.i386.rpm

mplayer-vidix-radeon-1.0pre3-1.i386.rpm

mplayer-vidix-rage128-1.0pre3-1.i386.rpm

mplayer-vidix-trident-1.0pre3-1.i386.rpm

mplayer-fb-1.0pre3-1.src.rpm

Optional fonts:

mplayer-font-cp1250-1.1-1.noarch.rpm

mplayer-font-iso1-1.1-1.noarch.rpm

mplayer-font-iso2-1.1-1.noarch.rpm

mplayer-font-iso7-1.1-1.noarch.rpm

mplayer-font-iso9-1.1-1.noarch.rpm

mplayer-font-koi8r-1.1-1.noarch.rpm

Optional skins:

mplayer-skin-AlienMind-1.0-2.noarch.rpm

mplayer-skin-avifile-1.5-2.noarch.rpm

mplayer-skin-Blue-1.0-2.noarch.rpm

mplayer-skin-BlueHeart-1.4-2.noarch.rpm

mplayer-skin-Blue-small-1.0-2.noarch.rpm

mplayer-skin-Canary-1.0-2.noarch.rpm

mplayer-skin-CornerMP-1.0-2.noarch.rpm

mplayer-skin-CornerMP-aqua-1.0-2.noarch.rpm

mplayer-skin-Cyrus-1.0-2.noarch.rpm

mplayer-skin-default-old-1.7-2.noarch.rpm

mplayer-skin-disappearer-1.0-2.noarch.rpm

mplayer-skin-gnome-1.1-2.noarch.rpm

mplayer-skin-hayraphon-1.0-2.noarch.rpm

mplayer-skin-hwswskin-1.0-2.noarch.rpm

mplayer-skin-krystal-1.0-2.noarch.rpm

mplayer-skin-mentalic-1.1-2.noarch.rpm

mplayer-skin-MidnightLove-1.5-2.noarch.rpm

mplayer-skin-neutron-1.4-2.noarch.rpm

mplayer-skin-Orange-1.0-2.noarch.rpm

mplayer-skin-phony-1.0-2.noarch.rpm

mplayer-skin-plastic-1.1.1-2.noarch.rpm

mplayer-skin-proton-1.1-2.noarch.rpm

mplayer-skin-QPlayer-1.0.2-2.noarch.rpm

mplayer-skin-slim-1.0-2.noarch.rpm

mplayer-skin-softgrip-1.0-2.noarch.rpm

mplayer-skin-trium-1.0-2.noarch.rpm

mplayer-skin-WindowsMediaPlayer6-1.2-2.noarch.rpm

mplayer-skin-xanim-1.5-2.noarch.rpm

mplayer-skin-xine-lcd-1.0-2.noarch.rpm

Optional encoder:

mencoder-1.0pre3-1.i386.rpm

Optional source:

mplayer-1.0pre3-1.src.rpm

Now that we have all the files, let's discuss installation briefly. The 1.0pre3 version of mplayer requires installation using the *–nodeps* option, as shown in the following code. Alternately, you could install all the required packages and only those codecs, fonts, and skins you desire.

```
# rpm -ivh --nodeps lame*
# rpm -ivh --nodeps mplayer*
```

Are we done yet? Unfortunately not, since you need to specify which video output driver you will use. Additionally, to make matters more interesting, the graphical player (*gmplayer*) uses its own configuration files, which you can edit by right-clicking on the program and selecting *Preferences*. For the command-line tool used by Web browsers, you can edit the file *~/.mplayer/config* so that it has the following line inside:

```
vo=x11
```

For *gmplayer* you can also select the X11 video output driver from the *Preferences* window under the *Video* tab. The available drivers are shown in Table 4.1.

Table 4.1   *Available gmplayer Drivers*

Xmga	Matrox G200/G4x0/G550
Xv	X11/Xv
x11	X11 (Ximage/Shm)
Xvidix	X11 (VIDIX)

While you can use other drivers if you have the appropriate hardware (Matrox and VIDIX), using the x11 driver will work on all machines and depends on your Xfree86 installation rather than on specific hardware.

Once everything is configured, you can launch *gmplayer* and, by right-clicking on the video box, you can use the menu option *DVD->Open Disk...* to open a DVD and play the default title on the DVD. If you wish to switch to another title, you can use the *DVD->Title* menu to switch between all known titles on the disk. Unlike other DVD players, there is no ability to use the DVD Menu associated with each DVD. You have to switch between the titles yourself.

4.1.7　How Do I Install the Mozilla Plugger Plug-in?

The Mozilla Plugger plug-in (http://fredrik.hubbe.net/plugger.html) is a glue layer that uses its own MIME-type definitions to load standard system viewers when content is accessed from the Web browsers. These viewers are then loaded using external windows and, in rare cases, embedded into Web page documents. Plugger needs to be built from source. The standard system viewers are tools that are installed with the OS and available from the command line. For example, the previously mentioned Xpdf could be considered a standard system viewer for acrobat files.

Building Plugger

```
# tar -xzf plugger-5.1.2.tar.gz
# cd plugger-5.1.2
[plugger-5.1.2]# ./configure
[plugger-5.1.2]# make
[plugger-5.1.2]# make install
```

After building Plugger you can then verify that Plugger is properly installed by using *Help->About Plug-ins* within Mozilla. You should see something similar to the image shown in Figure 4.7.

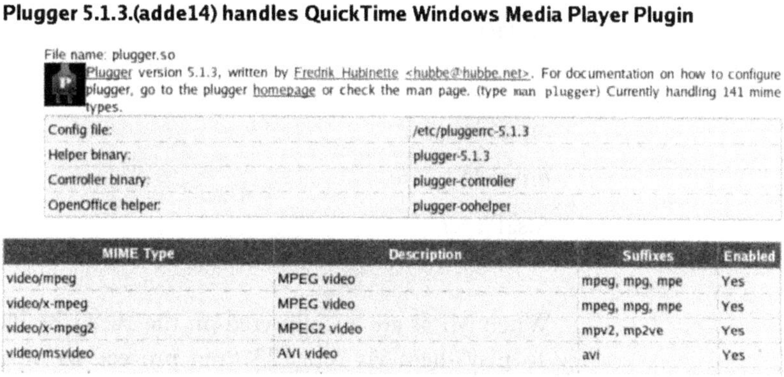

Figure 4.7
Mozilla plug-ins: Plugger installation.

Plugger 5.1.3.(adde14) handles QuickTime Windows Media Player Plugin

File name: plugger.so

Plugger version 5.1.3, written by Fredrik Hubinette <hubbe@hubbe.net>. For documentation on how to configure plugger, go to the plugger homepage or check the man page. (type man plugger) Currently handling 141 mime types.

Config file:	/etc/pluggerrc-5.1.3
Helper binary:	plugger-5.1.3
Controller binary:	plugger-controller
OpenOffice helper:	plugger-oohelper

MIME Type	Description	Suffixes	Enabled
video/mpeg	MPEG video	mpeg, mpg, mpe	Yes
video/x-mpeg	MPEG video	mpeg, mpg, mpe	Yes
video/x-mpeg2	MPEG2 video	mpv2, mp2ve	Yes
video/msvideo	AVI video	avi	Yes

As you can see, Plugger can display many multimedia formats and is the glue between multimedia content and the multimedia players. To verify that the plug-in is working correctly, visit the http://fredrik.hubbe.net/ plugger/test.html Web site and run through some of the test files. If some of the tests do not appear or play, then you will need to configure the necessary tools to make them play. Refer to Table 4.2 for information about which tool plays back which file format.

Plugger does odd things when it is in use; this is NOT a bug in the program, but the nature of the way Plugger uses Xfree86 to embed Windows within the Mozilla browser. The content may flash as a bigger window momentarily, before it appears within the browser. Do not be alarmed; this is by design. Last, if a Plugger program requires some form of setup to use, it is best to run that program outside of Mozilla before using it. A case in point is OpenOffice Writer (*oowriter*), since there are several windows used for configuration and registration. If you are unsure or concerned that the Plugger program is taking too long to load, first try the program outside Plugger.

Plugger has many capabilities, and we will look at these under their specific sections. Plugger does not produce output on its own, but uses third-party programs to produce that output. You must load some key programs onto your system to get the most out of your Plugger installation regarding multimedia. The most important is *mplayer*, discussed previously, while others are discussed in section 4.1.11.

4.1.8   How Do I Listen to MP3s?

Non-Web content can be listened to using many different MP3 players. There are many players, but the most common are:

KsCD (KDE)

mplayer

XMMS

mpg321

mpg123

AlsaPlayer

When MP3s are encountered on the Web, the Plugger plug-in will first try to play them via mpg123 then proceed to mpg321, mplayer, xmms, alsaplayer, amp, maplay, and then finally mpeg3player if the preceding players are not found. All of these tools can be used to play local as well as Web-based content. If you desire to use a saved playlist or *.m3u* file, then you are limited to the mpg123, mpg321, or xmms players.

There are issues with playing a playlist (*.m3u* file) via xmms from a Web browser using Plugger; however, *xmms* will play them just fine from the command line.

4.1.9 How Do I Display Streaming Media Web Content?

Quite a few streaming media formats are available outside RealPlayer, as discussed previously. A very common format is the Microsoft format used by Media Player, which we discuss next; however, there are so many formats and tools that Mozilla does not have enough plug-ins to display them all. Of note are the plug-ins necessary to watch virtual classroom media. The necessary plug-ins do not exist outside a Windows browser. But there is light at the end of the tunnel for these viewers, by using tools such as Cross-Over Office, VMware, and so forth. We describe these tools in detail in Chapter 5. If you are using Java-based Web tools, you are further limited to just Mozilla or VMware, since Java content will not display via Wine.

If, however, you wish to watch streaming movies, then the Plugger plug-in loads up mplayer to handle the content, or you can get the mplayer plug-in. For simplicity's sake, Plugger is the way to go; let it bring up the proper tool.

4.1.10 How Do I View or Listen to Microsoft Media Player Content?

To listen to Microsoft Media Player content you can use the Microsoft Media Player, which is only available via CrossOver Office and VMware. However, in many cases, mplayer will work just fine; you can even use the WMA plug-in for xmms.

CrossOver Office and VMware offer many features that can be used to display Microsoft proprietary application content and will be discussed in section 4.1.12.

4.1.11 How Do I View or Listen to Content of Various Types?

In nearly every case of viewing or listening to multimedia content, the Plugger plug-in will bridge the gap. Table 4.2 gives you the content type and which player will be used to view or listen to the specified MIME-type content. In some cases, more than one program can be used; the list is displayed in order of preference. For example, if you often play QuickTime content, you will need to have installed mplayer; if mplayer is not available, then xanim must be available to display this content. It should be noted that in some cases, Red Hat has removed certain functionality from the programs it supplies as a part of the base operating system due to copyright or legal concerns. xmms is one such program with certain limitations.

Table 4.2   *Content Types and Players Used to View/Listen to Them*

MIME Type	Description	Suffixes	Program
video/mpeg	MPEG video	mpeg, mpg, mpe	mplayer
video/x-mpeg	MPEG video	mpeg, mpg, mpe	mtvp
video/x-mpeg2	MPEG2 video	mpv2, mp2ve	xanim
video/msvideo	AVI video	avi	mplayer
video/x-msvideo	AVI video	avi	xanim
application/x-drm-v2	Windows Media	asx	
application/x-mplayer2	Windows Media	wmv, asf, mov	
application/x-mplayer2	WMV	wmv	
application/x-quicktimeplayer	Quicktime	mov	
video/x-ms-asf	Windows Media	asf, asx	
video/x-ms-asf-plugin	Windows Media	asf, asx, wma, wax, wmv, wvx	
video/x-ms-wm	MSNBCPlayer	asf	
video/x-ms-wmv	Windows Media	wmv	
video/x-ms-wvx	Windows Media	wvx	
video/sgi-movie	SGI video	movie, movi, mv	
video/x-sgi-movie	SGI video	movie, movi, mv	

Table 4.2 *Content Types and Players Used to View/Listen to Them (continued)*

MIME Type	Description	Suffixes	Program
video/x-theora	OGG stream with video		mplayer
video/theora	OGG stream with video		
video/ogg	OGG stream with video		
video/x-ogg	OGG stream with video	ogm, ogv	
video/quicktime	Quicktime video	mov, qt	mplayer
video/x-quick-time	Quicktime video	mov, qt	xanim
video/dl	DL video	dl	
video/x-dl	DL video	dl	
video/sgi-movie	SGI video	movie, movi, mv	
video/x-sgi-movie	SGI video	movie, movi, mv	
video/anim	IFF video	iff, anim5, anim3, anim7	
video/x-anim	IFF video	iff, anim5, anim3, anim7	
video/fli	FLI video	fli, flc	
video/x-fli	FLI video	fli, flc	
audio/mid	MIDI audio file	midi, mid	timidity
audio/x-mid	MIDI audio file	midi, mid	playmidi
audio/midi	MIDI audio file	midi, mid	
audio/x-midi	MIDI audio file	midi, mid	

Table 4.2   *Content Types and Players Used to View/Listen to Them (continued)*

MIME Type	Description	Suffixes	Program
audio/mp3	MPEG audio	mp3	mpg123 w/URL
audio/x-mp3	MPEG audio	mp3	mpg321
audio/mpeg2	MPEG audio	mp2	mplayer
audio/x-mpeg2	MPEG audio	mp2	mpg123 w/FILE
audio/mpeg3	MPEG audio	mp3	xmms
audio/x-mpeg3	MPEG audio	mp3	alsaplayer
audio/mpeg	MPEG audio	mpa, abs, mpega	amp
audio/x-mpeg	MPEG audio	mpa, abs, mpega	maplay
			mpeg3play
audio/mpeg-url	MPEG music resource locator	m3u	mpg123
audio/x-mpeg-url	MPEG music resource locator	m3u	mpg321
audio/mpegurl	MPEG music resource locator	m3u	xmms
audio/x-mpegurl	MPEG music resource locator	m3u	internal player
audio/mpeg-url	MPEG music resource locator	m3u	
audio/x-mpeg-url	MPEG music resource locator	m3u	
audio/x-scpls	Shoutcast Playlists	pls	
application/ogg	Ogg Vorbis stream	ogg	mplayer
application/x-ogg	Ogg Vorbis stream	ogg	xmms w/file
			ogg123
			xmms w/URL
			alsaplayer
audio/ogg	Ogg Vorbis audio stream	ogg	ogg123
audio/x-ogg	Ogg Vorbis audio stream	ogg	mplayer
			xmms
			alsaplayer

Table 4.2 *Content Types and Players Used to View/Listen to Them (continued)*

MIME Type	Description	Suffixes	Program
audio/x-pn-realaudio-plugin	RealPlayer Plugin Metafile	rpm	realplay
audio/x-pn-realaudio	Realaudio-plugin resource locator	ra, rm, ram	
audio/x-realau-dio	RealAudio file	ra, rm, ram	
application/ vnd.rn-realmedia	RealMedia file	rm	
application/smil	RealPlayer	smi	
audio/vnd.rn-realaudio	RealAudio file	ra, ram	
audio/vnd.rn-realvideo	RealVideo file	rv	
audio/basic	Basic audio file	au, snd	xanim
audio/x-basic	Basic audio file	au, snd	
audio/x-ms-wax	Windows Media	wax	mplayer
audio/wav	Microsoft wave file	wav	mplayer wavplay
audio/x-wav	Microsoft wave file	wav	bplay xmms
audio/x-pn-wav	Microsoft wave file	wav	xanim alsaplayer
audio/x-pn-win-dows-acm	Microsoft wave file	wav	playwave play
audio/mod	Soundracker audio Module	mod	mikmod tracker
audio/x-mod	Soundracker audio Module	mod	nspmod xmp alsaplayer

Table 4.2 *Content Types and Players Used to View/Listen to Them (continued)*

MIME Type	Description	Suffixes	Program
audio/prs.sid	SID Music	sid	sidplay
audio/x-sidtune	Commodore 64 audio	sid, psid, dat	
audio/sidtune	Commodore 64 audio	sid, psid, dat	
audio/psid	Commodore 64 audio	psid, sid, dat	
audio/x-psid	Commodore 64 audio	psid, sid, dat	
audio/x-stsound	Atari YM audio files	snd, psg, ym	stsoundc
audio/stsound	Atari YM audio files	snd, psg, ym	
image/tiff	TIFF image	tiff, tif	xvroot
image/x-tiff	TIFF image	tiff, tif	gqview
image/x-tif	TIFF image	tiff, tif	display (imagemagick)
image/sun-raster	Sun raster image	rs	sdtimage
image/x-sun-raster	Sun raster image	rs	qiv
image/x-rgb	RGB Image	rgb	
image/x-portable-pixmap	PPM Image	ppm	
image/x-portable-gray-map	PGM Image	pgm	
image/x-portable-bitmap	PBM Image	pbm	
image/x-portable-anymap	PBM Image	pnm	

Table 4.2   *Content Types and Players Used to View/Listen to Them (continued)*

MIME Type	Description	Suffixes	Program
application/photoshop	Photoshop Image	psd	xvroot
application/x-photoshop	Photoshop Image	psd	display (imagemagick)
			xli & imagemagick
			xloadimage & imagemagick
image/x-xcf	Gimp Image	xcf	xvroot
image/xcf	Gimp Image	xcf	display (imagemagick)
application/x-gimp	Gimp Image	xcf	xli & xcftopnm
			xloadimage & xcftopnm
application/gimp	Gimp Image	xcf	
application/pdf	PDF file	pdf	acroread
application/x-pdf	PDF file	pdf	gv
text/pdf	PDF file	pdf	xpdf
text/x-pdf	PDF file	pdf	
application/x-dvi	DVI file	dvi	xdvi
application/x-postscript	PostScript file	ps	gv
			ghostview
application/postscript	PostScript file	ps	pageview
			ghostscript

Table 4.2   *Content Types and Players Used to View/Listen to Them (continued)*

MIME Type	Description	Suffixes	Program
application/rtf	Rich Text Format	rtf	oowriter
application/x-msword	Microsoft Word Document	doc, dot	abiword
application/msword	Microsoft Word Document	doc, dot	sdtpcv
application/vnd.sun.xml.writer	OpenOffice.org Writer Document	sxw	
application/vnd.sun.xml.writer.template	OpenOffice.org Writer Template Document	stw	
application/vnd.sun.xml.writer.global	OpenOffice.org Writer Global Document	sxg	
application/vnd.stardivision.writer	StarWriter Document	sdw	
application/x-starwriter	StarWriter Document	sdw	
application/vnd.stardivision.writer-global	StarWriter Global Document	sgl	
application/wordperfect5.1	WordPerfect 5.1 Document	wp	

Table 4.2   *Content Types and Players Used to View/Listen to Them (continued)*

MIME Type	Description	Suffixes	Program
application/ vnd.ms-excel	Microsoft Excel Document	xls, xlb	oocalc gnumeric
application/ vnd.sun.xml.calc	OpenOffice.org Calc Document	sxc	sdtpcv
application/ vnd.sun.xml.calc. template	OpenOffice.org Calc Template Document	stc	
application/ vnd.stardivi- sion.calc	StarCalc Docu- ment	sdc	
application/x- starcalc	StarCalc Docu- ment	sdc	
application/ vnd.lotus-1-2-3	Lotus 1-2-3 Doc- ument	123, wk1	
application/ vnd.sun.xml.imp ress	OpenOffice.org Impress Docu- ment	sxi	ooimpress
application/ vnd.sun.xml.imp ress.template	OpenOffice.org Impress Template Document	sti	
application/ vnd.stardivi- sion.impress	StarImpress Doc- ument	sdd	
application/ vnd.stardivi- sion.impress- packed	StarImpress Packed Docu- ment	sdp	
application/x- starimpress	StarImpress Document	sdd	
application/ vnd.ms-power- point	Microsoft Power- Point Slideshow	ppt	

Table 4.2   *Content Types and Players Used to View/Listen to Them (continued)*

MIME Type	Description	Suffixes	Program
application/ vnd.sun.xml. draw	OpenOffice.org Draw Document	sxd	oodraw
application/ vnd.sun.xml. draw.template	OpenOffice.org Draw Template Document	std	
application/ vnd.stardivision. draw	StarDraw Document	sda	
application/x-stardraw	StarDraw Document	sda	
application/ vnd.sun.xml. math	OpenOffice.org Math Document	sxm	oomath
application/ vnd.stardivision. math	StarMath Document	smf	
application/x-starmath	StarMath Document	smf	
chemical/x-pdb	Protein Data Bank file	pdb	molecule (xscreen-saver)
model/x-pdb	Protein Data Bank file	pdb	

➤

Table 4.2   *Content Types and Players Used to View/Listen to Them (continued)*

MIME Type	Description	Suffixes	Program
model/vrml	Virtual Reality Modeling Language	vrl, vrml	vrweb
model/x-vrml	Virtual Reality Modeling Language	vrl	
world/vrml	Virtual Reality Modeling Language	vrl, vrml	
world/x-vrml	Virtual Reality Modeling Language	vrl	
x-world/vrml	Virtual Reality Modeling Language	vrl, vrml	
x-world/x-vrml	Virtual Reality Modeling Language	vrl	
application/x-troff-man	MAN pages	man	plugger-text via nroff

Some small changes need to be made to the */etc/pluggerrc-5.0* configuration file in order for some of the MIME types to work.

Video/MPEG requires the following change; it may be slow to load, since the removal of the *-cache* option will affect performance, but it will not abort prematurely. Make these lines:

```
embed url ignore_errors have(mplayer):sleep 99999999 | mplayer
-quiet -xy $xsize -wid $hexwindow -cache 1000 -vop pp -autoq 99
-nojoystick -nofs -zoom -osdlevel 1 "$url" >/dev/null 2>/dev/
null
noembed url ignore_errors have(mplayer) maxaspect
swallow(mplayer):sleep 99999999 | mplayer -quiet -cache 1000 -
vop pp -autoq 99 -nojoystick -nofs -zoom -osdlevel 1 "$url" >/
dev/null 2>/dev/null
```

Look like:

```
embed url ignore_errors have(mplayer):sleep 99999999 | mplayer
-quiet -xy $xsize -wid $hexwindow -vop pp -autoq 99 -nojoystick
-nofs -zoom -osdlevel 1 "$url" >/dev/null 2>/dev/null
noembed url ignore_errors have(mplayer) maxaspect
swallow(mplayer):sleep 99999999 | mplayer -quiet -vop pp -autoq
99 -nojoystick -nofs -zoom -osdlevel 1 "$url" >/dev/null 2>/
dev/null
```

In addition, you may need to install more files to get the complete functionality of Plugger. This truly depends on your package. At the very least you will need:

- TiMidity++ to play midi sound files. However, the TiMidity comes with RHEL3 as part of the kdemultimedia-3.1.3-1.rpm and therefore will only work if the aRts sound server is running. This server only runs when KDE is in use as a desktop.

- Xanim to play AU sound files. This package leaves a lot to be desired, since it has not been modified in years. Since it is only necessary to use Xanim to play .au files, it is best to use an alternative. If you use GNOME, you can use esdplay; if you use KDE, you can use artsplay to play these sounds. Since the use of a desktop is personal, we have to write a script to make the use of esdplay or artsplay be transparent. However, if the sox RPM is installed, then this is not needed, since the *play* command is available.

To do this, create a file named *sndplay* in */usr/local/bin*:

```
#/bin/sh
if [ x"$GDMSESSION" = x"GNOME" ]
then
    esdplay $*
elif [ x"$GDMSESSION" = x"KDE" ]
then
    artsplay $*
else
    echo "Unknown session"
fi
```

Then modify the */etc/pluggerrc-5.0* file so that the audio/x-basic MIME-type looks similar to the following:

```
audio/x-basic: au,snd: Basic audio file
   controls: play "$file"
   controls: sndplay "$file"
   loop: xanim +Av100 -Zr +W$window +q +f "$file"
```

This is also an advantageous thing to do for wav files, since the existing tools leave a lot to be desired; mplayer falls short in the playing of wav files.

- MikMod to play Soundtracker audio Module files. This is a part of the *mikmod-3.1.6-20.rpm* package, which is part of the RHEL3 installation media.

- sidplay to play Commodore 64 audio files. sidplay can be found at www.geocities.com/SiliconValley/Lakes/5147/sidplay. While there are two versions, you will need to build only sidplay; do not use the build sidplay2 release, since it does not work. The first step is to build the libraries, and the second to build the player:

```
# tar -xzf libsidplay-1.36.59.tgz
# cd libsidplay-1.36.59
# ./configure; make; make install
# cd ..
# tar -xzf sidplay-base-1.0.9.tar.gz
# cd sidplay-base-1.0.9
# ./configure; make; make install
```

4.1.12   How Do I View Microsoft Office Documents?

There are three primary Microsoft Office documents to be viewed via a Web browser: Excel, PowerPoint, and Word. While these documents are common to Microsoft Office, they are not always common to a Linux desktop. What you can see depends mostly on which features are required by the files you are viewing. In some cases, you may see something slightly different from what you expect. For example, graphs in Excel are not always where you expect them to be, and page breaks in Word can be unique, depending on the tool used. There are five possible tools to view these documents:

OpenOffice

This option is installed automatically when you install Plugger (see section 4.1.7). However, you should launch the OpenOffice tools outside the browser to agree to the license terms and configure the tools. Once you do this, the tools are available for use within Mozilla with no major issues. However, it should be restated that even though OpenOffice is a great tool, it is not from Microsoft; as a result, not everything will work as you might expect. The most benign problem may be incorrect fonts or bad page breaks. Other problems are missing graphics or incorrectly sized presentations. OpenOffice is improving continually but is always behind the software vendor.

For OpenOffice to work as part of the Plugger plug-in, you will first have to be sure the following RPMs are installed:

```
openoffice.org-libs-1.1.0-15.EL
openoffice.org-i18n-1.1.0-15.EL
openoffice.org-1.1.0-15.EL
```

While these package names are for RHEL3, the other distributions use similar names for their OpenOffice packages.

StarOffice

This for-fee product from Sun Microsystems costs roughly $80 and can either be purchased in CD-ROM form or as a download. While this suite of programs is similar to OpenOffice, it has different names for every program. Since Plugger v5.1.2 contains a preprocessor, you can safely switch between OpenOffice and StarOffice by setting your path so that the necessary programs precede the OpenOffice versions in the path (e.g., *swriter* vs. *oowriter*).

CrossOver Office

CrossOver Office ($59) provides an extremely nice suite of tools that allows you to run Microsoft Windows programs within your Linux installation using Wine. While Wine is extremely powerful and free, CrossOver Office is a for-fee tool that provides a clean method for installing your Windows programs into the underlying Wine layer, enabling you to run everything as you desire. In this way, you could run Internet Explorer instead of Mozilla. However, there are many limitations, since CrossOver Office and Wine do not support many of the necessary features required for a true Windows desktop.

One of the biggest benefits is that you will be able to run Internet Explorer directly, with almost all its standard plug-ins. One of the primary exceptions is the Java Virtual Machine; it is available, but it does not run appropriately, since it hangs the browser.

To install Internet Explorer follow the CrossOver Office–provided wizard.

CrossOver Plugin

CrossOver Plugin ($39) is a companion to CrossOver Office that modifies your Mozilla to use Wine and many of the existing Microsoft document readers available to view Microsoft media from your browser. This powerful tool gives great compatibility when viewing documents produced by the Microsoft Office suite of products, since it uses viewers written specifically by the vendor.

While CrossOver Plugin does not run Internet Explorer directly, it allows you to use all your Mozilla plug-ins as well as those specific to Microsoft Office, including Office document viewers and Media Player. To install these plug-ins, use the provided CrossOver Plugin wizard. Cross-Over Plugin has been merged into the CrossOver Office product and the same viewers can be enabled to view documents via the web.

VMware

VMware is another for-fee ($199) product that will place a Virtual Machine running Windows on your Linux desktop. Using this product grants you the ultimate in compatibility, because it runs a full-blown version of Windows inside your Linux desktop. With VMware, Internet Explorer and all its standard plug-ins are available. VMware will provide the highest level of compatibility. However, you also need a copy of Microsoft Windows to install into the virtual machine—yet another expense.

4.2   Web Publishing

In many ways publishing Web documents is both easier and more difficult when using Linux. In Linux, you have more ways to actually edit the documents, and less ways to interact with FrontPage-style servers used by the corporate network. In essence, there is no real equivalent to FrontPage in Linux, but there are some extremely nice tools that attempt to mimic this behavior.

We should point out the several advantages to using FrontPage that are not available when using many of the Linux tools. While most of these have alternatives, FrontPage and these alternatives do not work well together.

■ CVS, RCS, and SCCS are alternatives to FrontPage's check-out/in facility, but these cannot be used with FrontPage directly without a third-party plug-in.

■ Documents can be published to a FrontPage server even when the folder is not shared or mounted to the Linux box.

■ FrontPage plug-ins provide enhanced tools.

Taking these differences into consideration is a major concern for the administrator. If you want to edit documents on a Linux system and you cannot run FrontPage itself, there is no way to publish documents without mapping or mounting the FrontPage repository directly to the machine. You can download and save Web pages using many tools, but publication, FrontPage's major ability, is NOT available without direct access to the share.

Does your IT administrator want to grant this functionality? Be aware that once it is granted, the check-in/out functionality of FrontPage can be completely bypassed. The alternative is to use a different source code control system.

With this in mind, we can split the functionality between publishing (or placing the documents onto the Web server to be served) and editing the Web documents. Most editors can grab Web pages using a screen-scraping method, in which the document is downloaded into a placeholder and then allowed to be edited. However, the editors who do this can not edit dynamically created Web pages, and this will lead to confusion. Direct access to the files in question is really the better way to go, so you need some access to the file repository or a copy of all these files. Assuming we somehow have a local copy of the document, we can use a number of tools to do editing.

4.2.1 Mozilla

Mozilla's Web editing capabilities are quite nice, since it is a WYSIWYG editor; however, it only allows you to edit one page at a time, rather than viewing interactions between all the pages.

Figure 4.8

Figure 4.8
Mozilla Web Page Editor.

4.2.2 Quanta

Quanta is a sort of WYSIWYG editor, in that you can preview your work at any time. It comes the closest to the functionality of FrontPage on Linux, as you can upload files to servers using one of the supported mechanisms (smb, nfs, ftp, webdav, etc.). It also contains an HTML syntax checker that is extremely useful. However, the use of plug-ins is severely limited at this time, and you have to edit the HTML code directly.

4.2.3 Text Editor

While not a WYSIWYG editor for HTML, a text editor like vi or emacs can be one of the most powerful, since you can move files around quickly, as well as script the editing of many pages at once, which comes in very handy on major repetitive edits to files, such as changing company names or embedded copyright notices, and so on.

Alternately, you can use the following tools to run FrontPage directly and gain some of the benefits of its abilities.

4.2.4 CrossOver Office

CrossOver Office is a for-fee ($59) product that allows you to run FrontPage within a Linux system using the Windows emulator Wine. My testing of

Figure 4.9
*Quanta Web Page
Editor.*

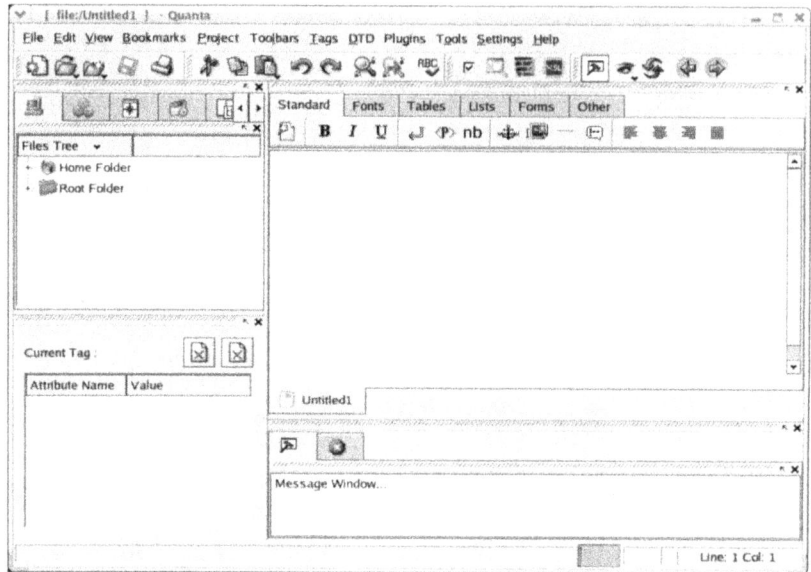

FrontPage through CrossOver Office showed many failures and crashes when accessing local files. Remote files cannot be accessed unless source code control systems are disabled, due to domain authentication issues.

4.2.5 VMware

VMware is another for-fee product ($199) that allows you to run the real FrontPage within a Windows Virtual Machine. Since VMware allows you to run as if you were on a Windows Machine, FrontPage has no limitations in its use.

4.3   The Cost

Using all these third party plugins on Linux is the same as using all the third party plugins on Windows. The costs are roughly the same. Outside of using CrossOver Office all the plugins come from many of the same places.

4.4   Support

Support for most of the plugins come from their respective vendors and the level of support is the same between Linux and Windows. The few exceptions are OpenOffice, and plugger, however, these Open Source projects are very active and responsive to problem reports.

4.5   Conclusion

All in all, Linux contains the necessary tools to browse web pages of all types and the tools necessary to edit them.Potential costs for Linux Web-browsing tools are displayed in Table 4.3.

Table 4.3   *Cost of Linux Replacements for Web-browsing Tools*

Software	Support Level	Fee	Support Fee
OpenOffice	OpenSource	NA	NA
StarOffice	Web-based/Phone	$80	Free for 60 days
VMware	Web-based/Phone	$199	Free for 90 days
Flash (macromedia)	Web-based	NA	NA
Mozilla	OpenSource	NA	NA
CrossOver Office	Web-based	$60	Free for 90 days
RealPlayer	Web-based	NA	NA
Acrobat (Adobe)	Web-based	NA	NA
Java (Sun or IBM)	Web-based	NA	NA

5

File Sharing

File sharing is an important feature of the desktop, so we will discuss ways of accessing file shares using CIFS (Common Internet File System), Apple-Talk, and NFS (Network File System) from the Linux desktop. We will also include a discussion about reading and writing different CD-ROM and hard disk formats.

When using CIFS and AppleTalk, there is an assumption that your desktop login will be your login to the file-sharing servers across the network. With Linux, this is not generally the case, but it can be with a properly configured *samba/ldap/kerberos* setup, so different approaches may be needed. We will cover standalone Linux, Wine, and VMware solutions to such file-sharing problems. Last, we will delve into how to read the myriad CD-ROM and hard disk formats in use today.

5.1 How Do I Authenticate against an Active Directory Server?

To authenticate against an Active Directory server, you must use the Kerberos system via the PAM security subsystem. Active Directory uses Kerberos to authenticate. There is, however, a caveat when using the *pam_krb5* module: you must be on the network first, so road warriors need to connect to the VPN before they can log in and authenticate against the AD server.

5.1.1 RHEL3

First ensure that the following RPMs are installed:

```
authconfig-gtk
pam_krb5
krb5-libs
krb5-workstation
```

Figure 5.1
*Red Hat
authentication
configuration
dialog box.*

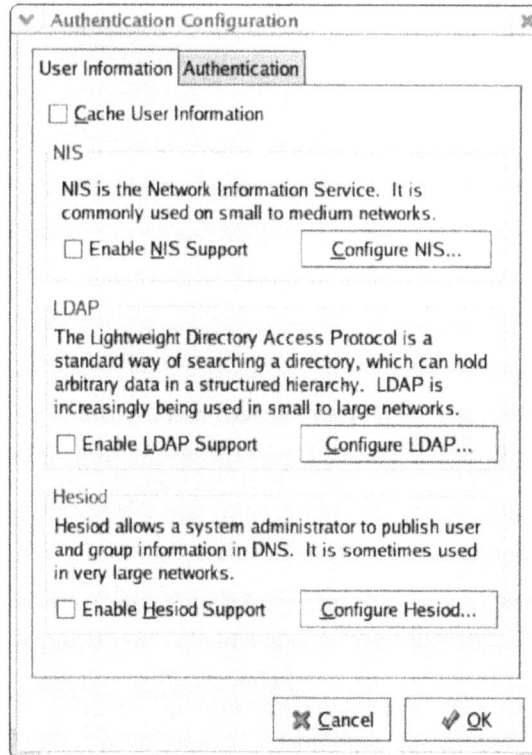

Then run:

redhat-config-authentication (as shown in Figure 5.1). For RHEL4 and Fedora the command is system-config-authentication.

Select the *Authentication* tab and check the *Enable Kerberos* box (as shown in Figure 5.2).

Then click *Configure Kerberos* (see Figure 5.3).

However, this graphical method will only get you halfway there.

RHEL/Fedora and others

The next part requires you to edit the Kerberos 5 (krb5) configuration files. While the Red Hat graphical interface will set up the PAM modules properly, you still need to configure the rest of the files by hand. The resulting /*etc/pam.d/system-auth* file will look like the following:

Figure 5.2
*Configuration:
Authentication tab
showing Kerberos
support enabled.*

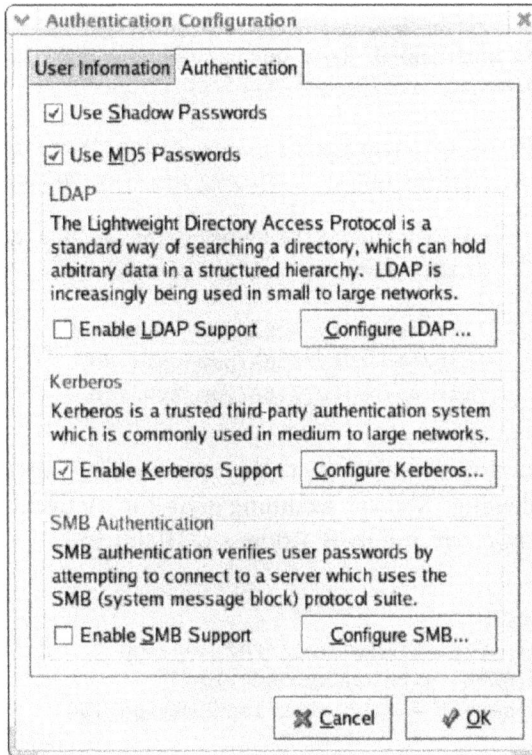

Figure 5.3
*Kerberos settings
dialog box.*

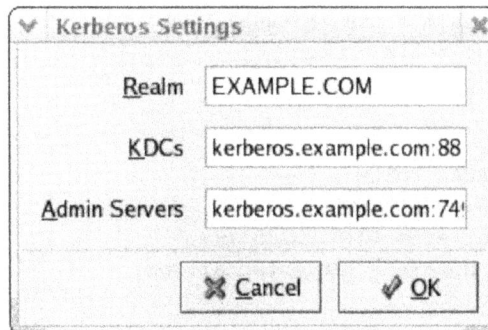

```
#%PAM-1.0
# This file is auto-generated.
# User changes will be destroyed the next time authconfig is run.
auth        required        /lib/security/$ISA/pam_env.so
auth        sufficient      /lib/security/$ISA/pam_unix.so likeauth nullok
auth        sufficient      /lib/security/$ISA/pam_krb5.so use_first_pass
auth        required        /lib/security/$ISA/pam_deny.so
```

```
account     required     /lib/security/$ISA/pam_unix.so
account     [default=bad success=ok user_unknown=ignore service_err=ignore
system_err=ignore] /lib/security/$ISA/pam_krb5.so

password    required     /lib/security/$ISA/pam_cracklib.so retry=3 type=
password    sufficient   /lib/security/$ISA/pam_unix.so nullok use_authtok md5
shadow
password    sufficient   /lib/security/$ISA/pam_krb5.so use_authtok
password    required     /lib/security/$ISA/pam_deny.so

session     required     /lib/security/$ISA/pam_limits.so
session     required     /lib/security/$ISA/pam_unix.so
session     optional     /lib/security/$ISA/pam_krb5.so
```

Next, you will need to modify your */etc/krb5.conf* file to be similar to the following. We are assuming that the Active Directory domain is *lab.internal.com* and its IP Address is 10.0.0.135.

```
[logging]
 default = FILE:/var/log/krb5libs.log
 kdc = FILE:/var/log/krb5kdc.log
 admin_server = FILE:/var/log/kadmind.log

[libdefaults]
 ticket_lifetime = 24000
 default_realm = LAB.INTERNAL.COM
 dns_lookup_realm = true
 dns_lookup_kdc = true

[realms]
 LAB.INTERNAL.COM = {
  kdc = 10.0.0.135:88
  admin_server = 10.0.0.135:749
  default_domain = lab.internal.com
 }

[domain_realm]
 .lab.internal.com = LAB.INTERNAL.COM
 lab.internal.com = LAB.INTERNAL.COM

[kdc]
 profile = /var/kerberos/krb5kdc/kdc.conf

[appdefaults]
 pam = {
```

```
    debug = false
    ticket_lifetime = 36000
    renew_lifetime = 36000
    forwardable = true
    krb4_convert = false
}
```

Finally, create the file */var/kerberos/krb5kdc/kdc.conf*, which may not already exist on your machine, since it is generally created when *krb5-server* is installed. The file will look like the following:

```
[kdcdefaults]
 acl_file = /var/kerberos/krb5kdc/kadm5.acl
 dict_file = /usr/share/dict/words
 admin_keytab = /var/kerberos/krb5kdc/kadm5.keytab
 v4_mode = nopreauth

[realms]
 LAB.INTERNAL.COM = {
  master_key_type = des-cbc-crc
  supported_enctypes = des3-cbc-sha1:normal des3-cbc-
sha1:norealm des3-cbc-sha1:onlyrealm des-cbc-crc:v4 des-cbc-
crc:afs3 des-cbc-crc:normal des-cbc-crc:norealm des-cbc-
crc:onlyrealm des-cbc-md4:v4 des-cbc-md4:afs3 des-cbc-
md4:normal des-cbc-md4:norealm des-cbc-md4:onlyrealm des-cbc-
md5:v4 des-cbc-md5:afs3 des-cbc-md5:normal des-cbc-md5:norealm
des-cbc-md5:onlyrealm des-cbc-sha1:v4 des-cbc-sha1:afs3 des-
cbc-sha1:normal des-cbc-sha1:norealm des-cbc-sha1:onlyrealm
 }
```

Now you are ready to log in to your Linux box using an Active Directory server for authentication. It should be noted that the setup of Single System Identification is a very complex subject and this is only a partial solution to that goal.

5.2   **How Do I Access CIFS Shares?**

CIFS shares are accessed using the SMB (Server Message Block) protocol, which is implemented using the Samba package on Linux and enables the sharing of files, printers, and serial ports.

The KDE and Gnome desktops contain tools to mount CIFS shares directly by specifying a URL in its simplest form: *smb://server/share*. Using this method requires a bit more knowledge of the format of the URL for those systems that require domains, users, and passwords. In addition, using something like Nautilus, a file system explorer, does not make the share available from the command line; however, the reverse is true: anything available to the command line is available to the graphical tools.

Here are a few things to consider when using Samba to access CIFS shares:

- Unlike share authentication on Microsoft Windows machines, Linux does not have a global and automatic way to authenticate against the share.

- The automatic authentication enjoyed by Microsoft Windows users either requires the relaxing of permissions on the server or the placement of passwords within a file on the Linux box.

- Every access to a network share requires separate authentication.

- Password maintenance of global shares becomes an issue.

5.2.1   Using a URL

The advantage to using a URL within a tool such as Nautilus is distinct, since the file explorer is great for copying and manipulating files. The following URL style will access the share via Nautilus:

```
smb://user@password:machine/share
```

Via Nautilus this will appear as shown in Figure 5.4.

It will ask for a password, since we did not supply one on the Location line, so the dialog box shown in Figure 5.5 also appears. But, you may have to enter your credentials twice.

Programs other than Nautilus that require access to a global share may not be able to access the data. For this you need a mount point or a named directory, where you will mount the share onto the existing file system.

Using a mount point as a place to mount the CIFS share is extremely useful for those shares that must be available for programmatic reasons. You can use *smbmount* and the credentials cache file to automate this functionality; however, the placement of a password in a file in clear text is anathema to most system administrators, so be extremely careful with permissions. The mount point can be created at boot time after the network is available,

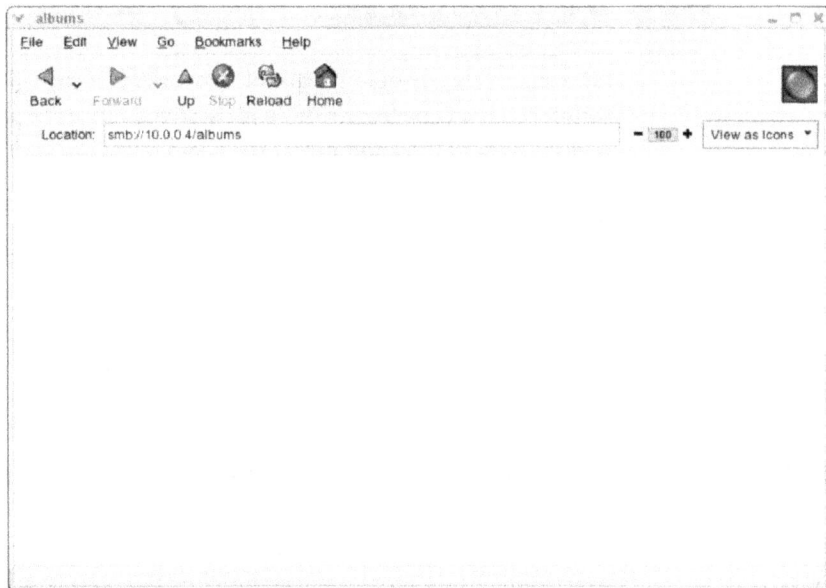

Figure 5.4
*Accessing the share
via Nautilus.*

or at login time. If you mount home directories, I suggest the login time
approach.

Issue the following command to mount a share. Note that the *.creden-
tials* file is the clear text file containing your username and password as documented via the smbmount manual page.

```
mount -t smbfs -o credentials=$HOME/.credentials //machine/
share <mount-point>
```

Figure 5.5
*Authentication
dialog box.*

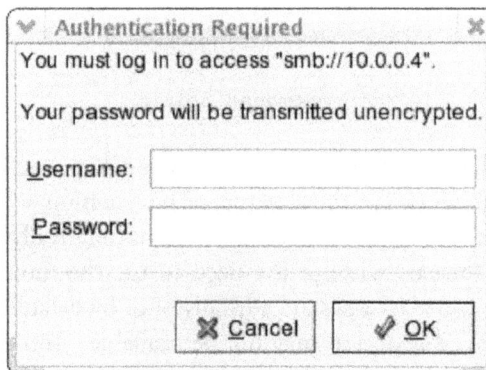

5.3   How Do I Access NFS File Systems?

NFS shares are the mainstream of network file sharing on Linux. Authentication is not a concern for these file systems, since the authentication model is at the system level and not at the user level. User access is governed by the standard Linux permissions. Mounts using NFS require mount points and root access to perform any mounts. If users need access to perform mounts, the *sudo* command, an alternative for logging into root that logs all root-based actions, can be used to perform the following mount command:

```
mount <directory@machine> <mount-point>
```

5.4   How Do I Access Macintosh Based Filesystems?

In some cases you will be required to access files that reside on a Macintosh computer. While most modern Macintosh computers speak either NFS or CIFS, there are older computers that speak AppleTalk. AppleTalk can be spoken by Linux using the netatalk package (http://netatalk.source-forge.net).

5.5   How Do I Access Various CD-ROM Formats?

The most commonly used CD-ROM format is ISO 9660, with or without extensions. ISO 9660 CD-ROMS are easily accessed using the mount command, and, depending on whether or not your system has been hardened, they will automatically be mounted to the desktop. The mount command to use is:

```
mount -o ro /dev/cdrom <mount-point>
```

Note that the mount point is a directory to which you have access. Modern Linux installations for the desktop or workstation will expose CD-ROM access functionality to the user and will automatically mount all common CD-ROM formats without the need to use the mount command which can only be issued by a system administrator by default. In the case of hardened systems, this option may not be available. You can use the information in Table 5.1 to access most common CD-ROM, floppy, or even hard disk formats. The command sequence when using this table is:

```
mount -o options -t type /dev/cdrom <mount-point>
```

When using Table 5.1 there are a few caveats. The first is that if you are using an ISO 9660 CD-ROM, you can simplify the command to:

```
mount -o options /dev/cdrom <mount-point>
```

A system administrator can set up the *letc/fstab* file to handle each of these formats so that automatic mounts happen. For floppy disks the /dev/fd0 device would be used in place of /dev/cdrom.

Table 5.1   *Accessing Common CD-Rom, Floppy and Hard Disk Formats*

Format	Type	Options
Multisession (older)	udf	ro
Multisession (modern)	ISO 9660	ro
CDRW	ISO 9660	rw
Macintosh (native)	hfs	ro
Macintosh	ISO 9660	ro
Linux (native)	ext2	ro
Linux	ISO 9660	ro
UNIX (native)	ufs	ro
UNIX	ISO 9660	ro

5.5 How Do I Access Other Disk Devices?

Let's look at some other formats of interest as well. For example, if the machine has Windows on one disk and Linux on another, you may have to access data from both disks, no matter how the machine is booted. If your Windows disk is NTFS, you can use the experimental NTFS disk format available to Linux; however, if you mount NTFS read/write instead of the suggested read-only, you run the risk of corrupting the hard disk. The NTFS and UFS read/write drivers must be compiled into your kernel first, which could void your distribution warranty as its is not a supported configuration.

The method of mounting is the same as a CD-ROM; however, you will have to determine which the disk device to use. If access to the disk is a regular activity on your Linux desktop, you will also want to add an entry into your *letc/fstab* file to automatically mount the disk on boot. Table 5.2 continues from Table 5.1, and the same style of mount commands are available.

Table 5.2 *Accessing Other Disk Devices*

Format	Type	Options
NTFS (hard disk)	ntfs	ro/rw
Compact Flash	vfat	rw
UNIX (native)	ufs	ro/rw

There are many ways to determine which hardware is available to your machine by default. In this search, I check the output of the *mount* command to determine which devices are automatically mounted or made available to me. If the device is not in this list, then we proceed to different mechanisms. Since we are only looking for disk devices, the mount command will tell us all the currently mounted disk devices. Many of the lines can be ignored as not useful, but the key ones are the partitions */dev/hda2* and */dev/hda1*, which all belong to the */dev/hda* disk.

```
/dev/hda2 on / type ext3 (rw)
none on /proc type proc (rw)
none on /dev/pts type devpts (rw,gid=5,mode=620)
usbdevfs on /proc/bus/usb type usbdevfs (rw)
/dev/hda1 on /boot type ext3 (rw)
none on /dev/shm type tmpfs (rw)
```

This result tells us that only */dev/hda* is currently mounted.

5.5.1 RHEL3

Since we want to determine which other devices can be mounted, we can review the output of the *hwbrowser* command, which displays all the currently active devices available. Once you run the command, a dialog box will appear, as shown in Figure 5.6.

The Hardware browser will open to your current CD-ROM drive. To determine the other disk devices available, click on *Hard Drives* and they will be displayed (as shown in Figure 5.7). In this case, I wanted to find out the disk device for my compact flash card, which is loaded into the PCM-CIA slot.

Figure 5.6
Hardware browser
dialog box.

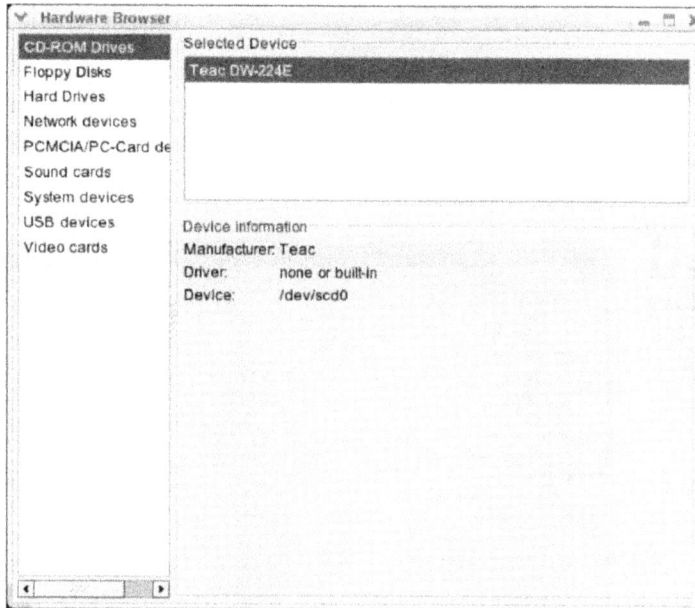

Figure 5.7
Hardware browser
dialog box,
checking for
available hard
drives.

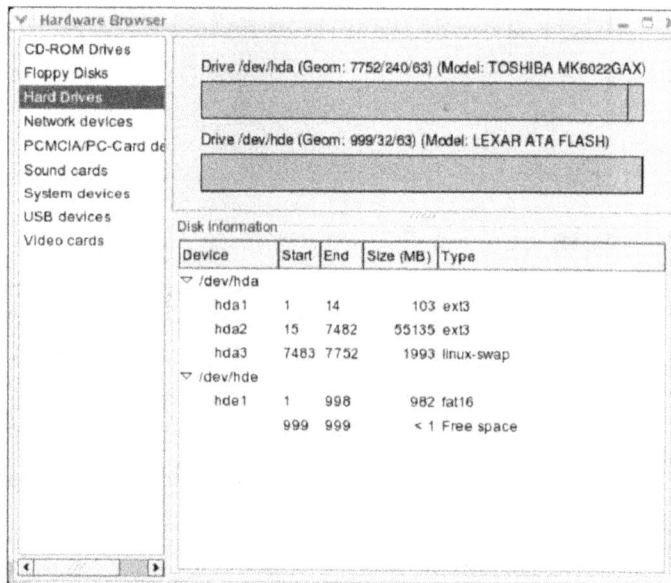

In Figure 5.7, you can see that the device I want is the *hde* device, specifically the */dev/hde1* device and partition.

5.5.2   **Mandrake**

Similar to *hwbrowser* is the *harddrake2* command, which appears in Figure 5.8; it will show you the exact device necessary to use in the left column. Clicking on the device will show you the device and partition necessary for a mount to occur.

Figure 5.8
Harddrake dialog box.

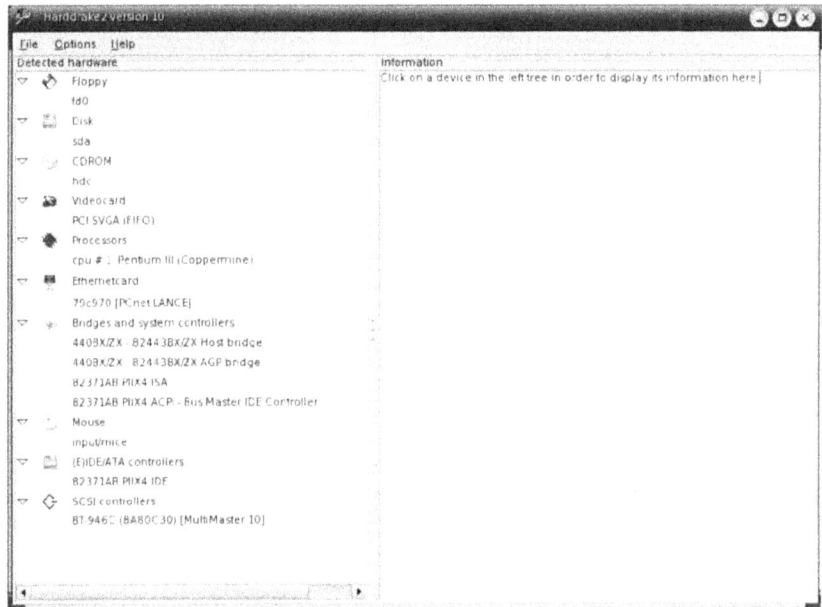

SuSE

SuSE uses its own Hardware browser, which is different from the others. It will present similar to the following after starting YaST and selecting Hardware Information from the right hand side. Once the Hardware Information dialog is opened you can scroll down and expand the Disk section to show the device associated with each disk drive (see Figure 5.9).

Now that this information is available, we can move forward with the appropriate command:

```
mount —t vfat /dev/hde1 /mnt
```

If for some reason the Hardware browser (for your Linux installation) does not show your devices, you can then refer to the output of *dmesg* to determine the available devices, using this:

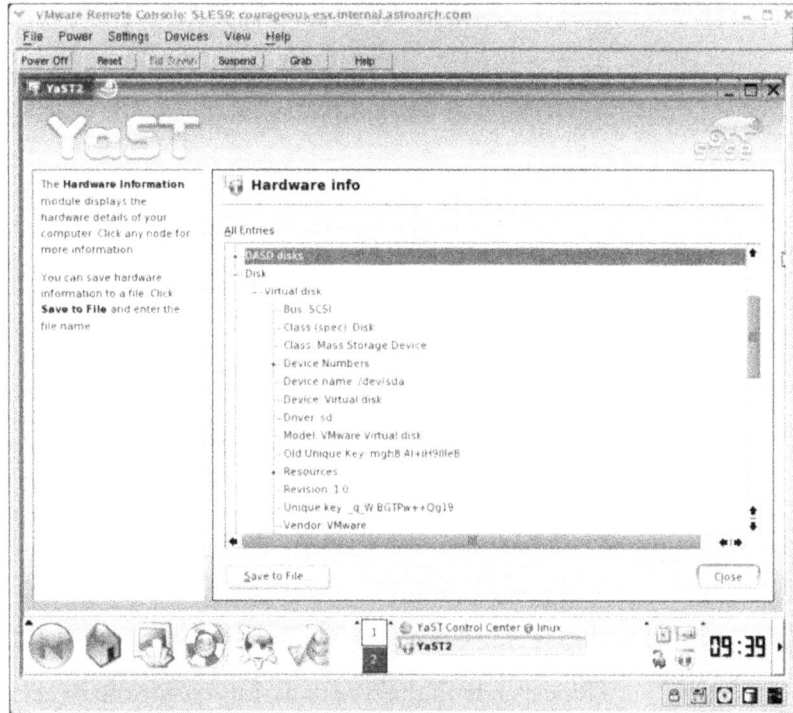

Figure 5.9
*YaST Hardware
Browser.*

```
# dmesg | egrep 'hd|sd'
hde: LEXAR ATA FLASH, CFA DISK drive
hde: attached ide-disk driver.
hde: task_no_data_intr: status=0x51 { DriveReady SeekComplete
Error }
hde: task_no_data_intr: error=0x04 { DriveStatusError }
hde: 2014992 sectors (1032 MB) w/1KiB Cache, CHS=1999/16/63
 hde: [PTBL] [999/32/63] hde1
ide_cs: hde: Vcc = 3.3, Vpp = 0.0
```

If *dmesg* is not available and you have root access, you can look into the *syslog* messages file as well:

```
egrep 'hd|sd' /var/log/messages
```

The output provided also shows me that device *hde*—and specifically */dev/ hde1*—is the device I should use in my mount command. Use of *sd* in the command will also show any SCSI devices which is generally how USB disks show up.

5.6   How Do I Make Image Files from a CD-ROM?

Making an image of a CD-ROM is extremely straightforward in command syntax, but not when finishing the image. To make the CD-ROM image, use:

```
dd if=/dev/cdrom of=<image file>
```

or

```
readcd dev=/dev/cdrom f=<image file>
```

However, some CD-ROM devices have problems trying to find the end of the device, and a subsequent read failure must occur before you physically eject the CD-ROM, which could make the system appear to hang until the CD-ROM is ejected. Granted, this has only been experienced using a DVD drive on older kernels.

5.7   How Do I Create a CD-ROM?

This depends on the type of device you want to be able to read the resulting CD-ROM. The base command is *cdrecord*, and it has many options. However, creating a disk is a three-step process.

1. Place all the files that you would like to burn to disk into one directory.

2. Use the *mkisofs* command to create an ISO image of that directory.

3. Use *cdrecord* to record the resulting ISO image to the CD-ROM device.

Table 5.3   *Options for Command mkisofs*

Format	Type	Options	*cdrecord* Options
ISO9660	iso9660	-J -R	
Multisession	udf/iso9660		-multi
Macintosh	hfs	-hfs	
UNIX	ufs/ext2	None, use *cdrecord* directly on the device	

mkisofs is the important command, and it has many options, as shown in Table 5.3.

Refer to Table 5.3 and run the following commands:

```
cd temporary_data_directory
mkisofs options -o /tmp/output.iso .
cdrecord options /tmp/output.iso
```

It is possible to make very complex images with *mkisofs* that boot and display different data, based on the OS used to read the CD-ROM, the mkisofs manual page contains these complex examples. Last, Nautilus can also be used to burn images to the CD-ROM device using a the burn://... location will create a standard ISO9660 image, while you can use the following commands to do the same:

```
cd path_to_dir_to_burn
mkisofs -J -R -o /tmp/output.iso .
cdrecord /tmp/output.iso
```

5.8 How Do I Make Bootable CD-ROMs?

Bootable CD-ROMs are often a requirement for making recovery CD-ROMs. These very useful CD-ROMs will assist an administrator in recovering a system or even to perform forensics on a system at will. Granted, the distribution media can always be used, but why keep a seven-CD-ROM set handy when a business card–sized CD-ROM will give the ability to boot from CD and thereby allow access to the machine for administrative purposes. To build a bootable CD-ROM you will need to have the syslinux RPM installed.

5.8.1 RHEL3

```
up2date syslinux
```

Once *syslinux* is installed, you can make your CD-ROM, using the following instructions:

```
mkdir iso
cd iso
mkdir isolinux
```

```
cp —r /usr/lib/syslinux/isolinux.bin isolinux
cp files . # copy all your necessary files to this directory
including any commands you wish to run and libraries to run
these commands including your kernels etc.
# note that there is much more involved in making a bootable
cdrom including the necessary kernel files and config files not
covered here.
mkisofs —J —T —v —r —c isolinux/boot.cat —b isolinux/
isolinux.bin —no-emul-boot —boot-load-size 4 —boot-info-table —
o ../file.iso
```

Please note that this is by no means complete; this example demonstrates only the basics and the necessary *mkisofs* command. If you want to make a recovery CD-ROM, there is a very promising project called *mkcdrec* (www.mkcdrec.org) that will guide you through making a bootable recovery CD-ROM (for the recovery of your system from backup media, or just to boot the system in case the master boot record is destroyed) or any other form of bootable CD-ROM. Included in this project is necessary steps to create a bootable CD-ROM including any necessary drivers and presents an all inclusive package that can be added to easily. Since this project is designed to make a recover CD-ROM it is all that is necessary to aid in the situation discussed. In addition there is the mkbootdisk command which will create boot disk specific to your system, for example:

```
mkbootdisk --device /tmp/bootdisk.iso --iso `uname -r`
cdrecord /tmp/bootdisk.iso
```

The mkbootdisk manual page will contain more details.

5.9   How Do I Manipulate Floppy Disks?

Floppy disks, like CD-ROMs, come in multiple formats. However, the most prevalent is the DOS format. To manipulate a DOS format disk, first make sure that the mtools package is installed.

```
RHEL: rpm -q mtools
```

mtools provides tools that emulate the DOS commands that you would normally use, except these commands are preceded with an *m*; *format* becomes *mformat*, *copy* becomes *mcopy*, *dir* becomes *mdir*, *cd* becomes *mcd*, and so forth. It should be noted that most text files will need to be translated from DOS to Linux using:

```
dos2unix < <inputfile> > <outputfile>
```

and then using the following when there is a need to give the text file back for a DOS user to use the disk contents once more:

```
unix2dos < <inputfile> > <outputfile>
```

The alternative type of floppy disk is the disk that holds a different type of file system. Use the standard mount commands to mount the file system, and then all standard Linux commands will work as expected.

5.10 The Cost

There is only one hidden cost involved, and that only applies if you need to manipulate esoteric file systems. This hidden cost is the cost of support if you must recompile your kernel to gain access to these file systems. However, if you stick to the standard kernels, many of these file systems are available by default in their benevolent forms. If you desperately need to manipulate NTFS partitions on the local machine, it may be appropriate to use a system such as VMware to create a real Microsoft Windows installation, instead of using the risky NTFS Write-enabled code in Linux. Once you use something like VMware, you can either set up a CIFS share to share the disk to the Linux server. This last option can be expensive and not generally necessary.

The costs are displayed in Table 5.4.

Table 5.4 *Cost of Linux Replacements for File-sharing Tools*

Software	Support Level	Fee	Support Fee
VMware	Web-based/Phone	$199	Free for 90 days
Kernel Modifications	None	Warranty voided	Warranty voided

6

Messaging

The instant communication tools necessary to communicate with your corporate colleagues continue to increase in importance. If you are a road warrior, being able to chat with your colleagues in real time while talking on the phone or with a customer can be a critical time saver and productivity booster. We will examine Linux-enabled tools for accessing Internet Relay Chat (IRC) servers and the AIM, Yahoo!, Microsoft (MSN), ICQ, and Jabber networks for speedy communication from your desktop.

6.1 IRC

One of the oldest network communication tools is (IRC) Internet Relay Chat, which provides group-to-peer and peer-to-peer communication via an IRC server somewhere on the network. While this tool is relatively insecure, it does provide a ready method for individuals and teams to communicate instantaneously. Most IRC clients provide the same features.

For example, we find that color-coded text, operations that perform automatically on startup of the client, and timestamps are invaluable; other people feel pop-up notifications and sounds are the most important features; and still others want their clients to have out-of-band file transfers available. There are many client-side features available to as many IRC clients, such as Xchat, ChatZilla, and mIRC.

6.1.1 Xchat

The Xchat tool provides an extensible graphical interface into an IRC server, with all the bells and whistles anyone could desire: notifications via color-coding, pop-up, and sounds. The interface is shown in Figure 6.1.

Figure 6.1
Xchat interface.

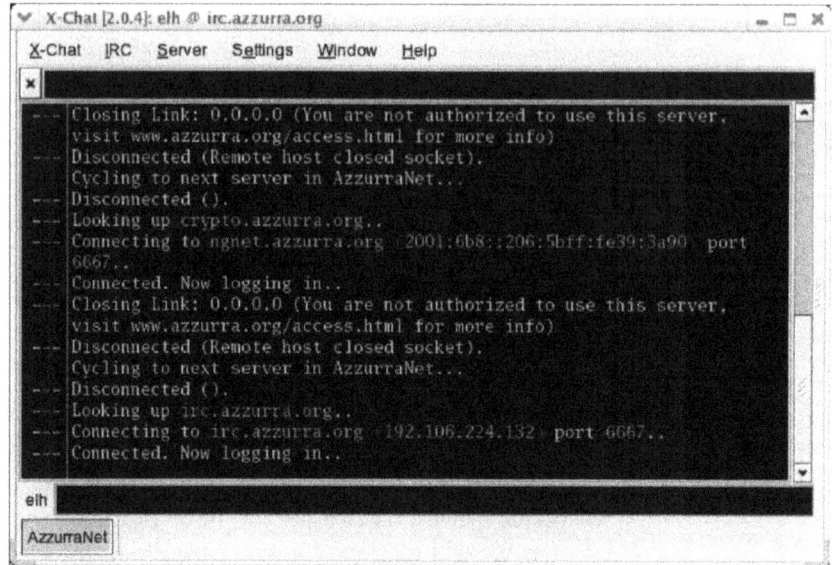

RHEL

```
up2date xchat
xchat &
```

6.1.2 ChatZilla

The ChatZilla tool is provided as a part of the Mozilla Web browser, and has many of the required features as well, except timestamped messages. However, ChatZilla does host a more aggressive style of highlighting and notifications. You can access ChatZilla from the Mozilla tools menu. The interface is shown in Figure 6.2.

6.1.3 mIRC

mIRC is a very common Windows-based client that can be run on the Linux desktop using either CrossOver Office ($79) or VMware ($199). While CrossOver Office or Wine provides Linux users with a method to run mIRC, some of the program's sound notification features may not work. Once mIRC is installed into CrossOver Office (Appendix A), you will need to create a menu item for it using the following code so that you can launch the program easily.

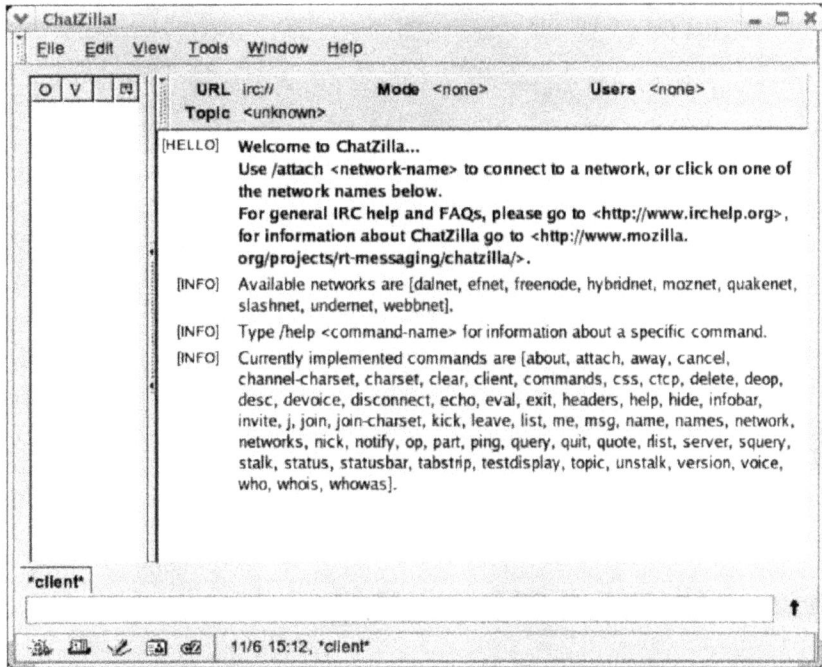

Figure 6.2
*ChatZilla
interface.*

```
cd .gnome2/vfolders/applications
cat > CXTree-Windows_Applications-Programs-mIRC.desktop <<EOF
[Desktop Entry]
Encoding=Legacy-Mixed
Type=Application
X-Created-by=cxoffice
Name=mIRC
Comment=mIRC
Exec=/opt/cxoffice/bin/wine --check --cx-app "C://Program
Files//mIRC/MIRC.EXE"
Icon=/home/elh/.cxoffice/dotwine/fake_windows/Windows/Icons/
cnf.xpm
Categories=Application;X-cxoffice;X-CXTree-
Windows_Applications-Programs;
EOF
```

While mIRC will run quite well, plug-ins may not run, so be sure to test thoroughly.

The mIRC interface is shown in Figure 6.3.

Figure 6.3
mIRC interface.

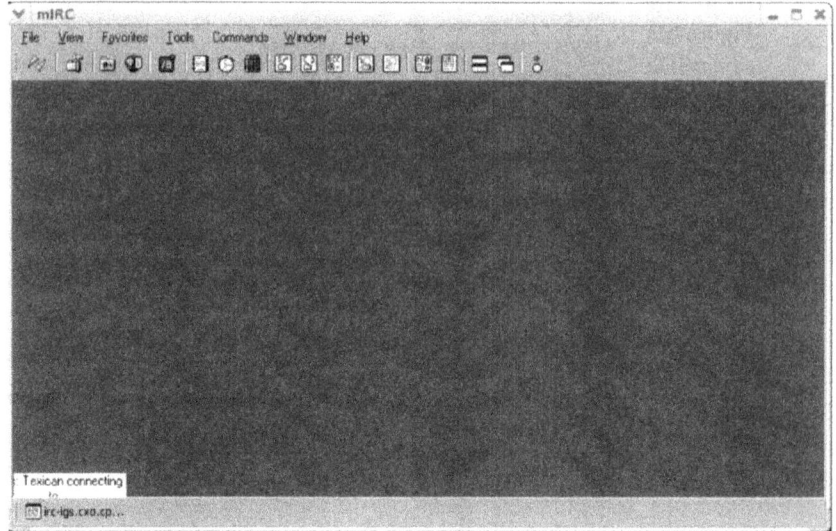

6.2   Video Conferencing

There are a few methods for video conferencing while using Linux; unfortunately, they do not interoperate very well. The first is Gnome Meeting, and the second is Microsoft's NetMeeting via CrossOver Office. Other tools are available to provide pictures or videos to users, but these are generally peer-to-peer tools and do not provide true video-conferencing capability. The OpenH323 Project (http://www.openh323.org) is an excellent place to start researching video conferencing.

6.2.1   GnomeMeeting

GnomeMeeting is a great tool that mimics the abilities of NetMeeting, yet shares none of its more useful protocols. Work is being done to achieve these protocols, but they have yet to be realized. Use of GnomeMeeting is therefore limited to video sharing with NetMeeting; there is no chat, application, or whiteboard sharing (T.120 Protocol). However, whiteboard and chat sharing are available for Linux-to-Linux hosts. To show video, you will need a video camera that uses Video4Linux drivers, which includes many Creative and Philips cameras, as well as a few Logitech cameras. A host of information is available at http://www.gnomemeeting.org. Also, the site http://www.exploits.org/v4l/ hosts a list of working drivers for Video4Linux-supported cameras. Some webcam support for Linux is disappearing while others

Figure 6.4
GnomeMeeting

are appearing. As with any Open Source project review the available list of supported hardware before purchasing.

Those people familiar with NetMeeting will find using GnomeMeeting just as comfortable. GnomeMeeting also has support for Voice over IP via MicroTelco Internet Telephone services (http://www.microtelco.com).

GnomeMeeting is installed as part of most modern versions of Linux and will look like Figure 6.4.

RHEL

```
up2date gnomemeeting
```

6.2.2 NetMeeting

Microsoft NetMeeting is also available when using CrossOver Office ($79) or via VMware ($199). VMware will provide the full NetMeeting functionality while CrossOver Office will not provide good sound or video capabilities, yet the chat, whiteboard, and application sharing all work. While Netmeeting is running it will allow you to view shared applications, it can not start the sharing process. Once NetMeeting is installed into CrossOver Office, you will need to create a menu item for it using the following:

```
cd .gnome2/vfolders/applications
cat > CXTree-Windows_Applications-Programs-NetMeeting.desktop
<<EOF
```

```
[Desktop Entry]
Encoding=Legacy-Mixed
Type=Application
X-Created-by=cxoffice
Name=NetMeeting
Comment=NetMeeting
Exec=/opt/cxoffice/bin/wine --check --cx-app "C://Program
Files//NetMeeting//CONF.EXE"
Icon=/home/elh/.cxoffice/dotwine/fake_windows/Windows/Icons/
cnf.xpm
Categories=Application;X-cxoffice;X-CXTree-
Windows_Applications-Programs;
EOF
```

Now you can launch NetMeeting from the Red Fedora menu and will present per figure 6.5. It should be noted that the most recent version of CrossOver office and the Internet Explorer installation includes a version of Netmeeting.

Figure 6.5
NetMeeting.

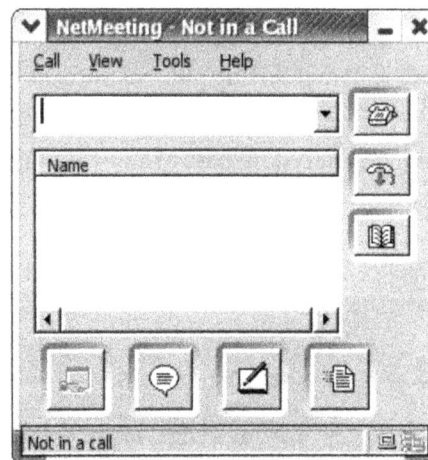

If you require video conferencing only, then both NetMeeting and GnomeMeeting will work. However, if you require training or a desktop-sharing environment, then NetMeeting is the only real tool.

6.3   Instant Messaging

Another widely used communication tool is Instant Messaging (IM). These tools work using servers that connect individuals to individuals and in some cases will connect groups of people as well. While not a true peer-to-peer network, the use of servers allows some store-and-forward capabilities and guarantees the protocols. Popular IM protocols are AIM, ICQ, MSN, Jabber, and Yahoo!. On Linux, each of these protocols has a client and sometimes two or three versions, ranging from command-line versions to very nice graphical clients. Table 6.1 contains a list of Linux clients available for each protocol.

Table 6.1   *Linux Instant Messaging Tools by Protocol*

Tool	Protocol	Web Site	Notes
Licq	ICQ	http://www.licq.org	Command-line tool
Gaim	AIM/MSN/Yahoo!/ ICQ	http://gaim.sourceforge.net	Graphical client available with most Linux systems
Yahoo!	Yahoo!	http://messenger.yahoo.com	Graphical client from Yahoo!
Ayttm	AIM/MSN/Yahoo!/ ICQ/Jabber	http://ayttm.sourceforge.net	Graphical client with encryption modules
EB-lite	AIM/MSN/Yahoo!/ ICQ/Jabber	http://www.everybuddy.com/eb-lite	Useful for WAP devices, including Java-based cell phones and PDAs

Most of the clients listed are universal clients, designed to have one client speak all the available protocols, which will save on screen real estate. However, they all have different design criteria. Choosing one depends on how you wish to use the client. For some, third-party for-fee plug-ins can be found, while for others these are not allowed. It all depends on the license in use.

6.3.1   EB-lite

EB-lite's philosophy is to create a server that speaks all the protocols and then allow clients to talk to that server. There are currently clients for PalmOS devices, cell phones, Linux Qt, Java, and command line via a Curses front end. There are also plans for a robust Windows front end.

6.3.2   Ayttm

Ayttm's philosophy is to create a monolithic client that has many plug-ins for its features. Currently there are plug-ins for SMTP, encryption (both GPG and proprietary RSA based), each protocol (and other esoteric protocols including IRC), notes, and translation tools. Ayttm even has a Windows version of its interface. Ayttm has support for the Yahoo! Webcam protocols, for peer-to-peer video conferencing.

6.3.3   Gaim

Gaim's philosophy is similar to Ayttm, and it is pretty much an active competitor to the project. It is missing Yahoo! Webcam support, but it does have scripting ability via Perl.

6.4   Peer-to-Peer Video Sharing

Outside of GnomeMeeting, NetMeeting via CrossOver Office, and Ayttm with its Yahoo! Webcam support, a few other tools are available for peer-to-peer video sharing. The current list of available tools includes programs such as nv, QSeeMe, and very few others. These tools either do not exist anymore or have not been updated recently. The most effort has gone into making GnomeMeeting work. Multiple items are needed to allow video, and although Linux does not support every device, it is supporting a growing number of devices. First you should find a device that will work on Linux, which implies that there is a device driver for the camera available. To show video, you will need a video camera that uses Video4Linux drivers, which includes many Creative and Philips cameras, and a few Logitech cameras. A host of information is available at http://www.gnomemeeting.org. http://www.exploits.org/v4l/ is a site that lists working drivers for Video4Linux-supported cameras and tools for sharing video over the Web. Ayttm uses JasPer (http://www.ece.uvic.ca/~mdadams/jasper/) to transmit images to other webcam clients.

6.5   The Costs

Outside of using either CrossOver office or VMWare there are no major costs outside of Linux supported web cameras. It should be noted that if Gnome Meeting is used for Voice over IP there will be VoIP fees as well.

6.6 Support

Support for the various Linux based tools is based on the Open Source communities and with the exception of some of the Instant Messenger Clients, all are quite active and responsive. Not having T.120 Protocol support in Gnome Meeting limits its effectiveness for meetings between Windows and Linux workstations.

While there are many useful IRC clients, there are not many meeting or training tools. Others outside of Netmeeting will be discussed in chapter 10.

6.7 Conclusion

There are many useful Linux based messaging tools available and only for items like Netmeeting is an alternative tools required. The costs are displayed in Table 6.2.

Table 6.2   *Cost of Linux Replacements for Video-Conferencing Tools*

Software	Support Level	Fee	Support Fee
VMware	Web-based/Phone	$199	Free for 90 days
CrossOver Office	Web-based/e-mail	$70	Free for 90 days
Webcams	Limited support	See vendor	Different by vendor; not many vendors support Linux outright
VoIP	Limited support	NA	NA

7

Terminal Emulators and Server Clients

It may become necessary to access command line shells, or legacy terminal-based applications running on other systems. To do this, you will need a character cell terminal client. In many cases, such access provides unique challenges, such as using the proper keyboard layout or terminal emulation mode. In other cases, you may just need to display Graphical Windows back to your machine using a Terminal Server client from a Windows based server.

7.1   How Do I Access Legacy-based Mainframe Programs?

To access legacy mainframe programs you will need a terminal emulator that can talk to the mainframe. There are many such tools available for use. We will review two mainframe systems and their corresponding clients.

First there is the IBM mainframe client. A tn3270 client will interact with IBM MVS-based mainframes and provide all the necessary features, including function key mappings for PC-style keyboards as necessary. There are a huge number of tn3270 clients available and we mention the class herein instead of the specific programs. tn3270 clients have one thing in common and that is that they will interact as if it was a 3270 terminal. While you may still be able to find a 3270 physical terminal, the tn3270 class of emulators are more prevalent and it is very difficult to choose which one is better than another so no emulators will be presented. They all have a few things in common including a method to input the specialized keys of a 3270 Terminal without requiring a modification to any other software on the system. While tn3270 emulators do not require the keymap to change other terminal programs do have this requirement.

Of critical importance when dealing with keyboards and XFree86 is the concept of a keyboard map that represents each key on the keyboard. While there is a keymap for the keyboard, there is a keycap definition for each individual key of the keymap (keyboard). By modifying keycaps, we can modify the way the keymap reports the press of keys on the keyboard. The program xmodmap will read a keymap file with its defined keycaps and modify the keymap of the running system.

For Digital (HP) VMS-based systems, you will need a VT400 terminal emulator. There are several VT400 terminal emulators, with the most convenient one already a part of all distributions. That tool is xterm.

7.1.1 RHEL

```
up2date xterm
```

While old-fashioned, xterm (when using the –sb) will place the numeric keypad into application mode rather than system mode and extend the keyboard map to handle function keys through 20, which is required by a VT400 terminal emulator.

If your keyboard does not support 20 function keys and these keys are necessary, you will need to map these keys using xmodmap or the XKey-Caps (http://www.jwz.org/xkeycaps/) graphical client, which will write out a file readable by xmodmap. For example, your keymap change will affect xterm as well as openoffice and any other application running at the time of the keyboard change and any future application. This is NOT a localized change. For example, you can use xmodmap/XKeyCaps to map ctrl-F3 through ctrl-F10 to be F13 through F20 using a keymap created using XKeyCaps. First, we need to build XKeyCaps, as it is much easier to manipulate xmodmap files using this tool.

7.1.2 Building XKeyCaps

```
# tar –xzf xkeycaps-2.46.tar.Z
# cd xkeycaps-2.46
# xmkmf
# make
# make install
```

7.1.3 Running XKeyCaps

```
# xkeycaps
```

```
# choose your keyboard from the list, it is older code so
choose closest match

# right click on key on keyboard to raise menu and select Edit
KeySyms of Key
```

The "Edit Key" dialog screen is shown in Figure 7.1.

Figure 7.1
"Edit Key" dialog
screen.

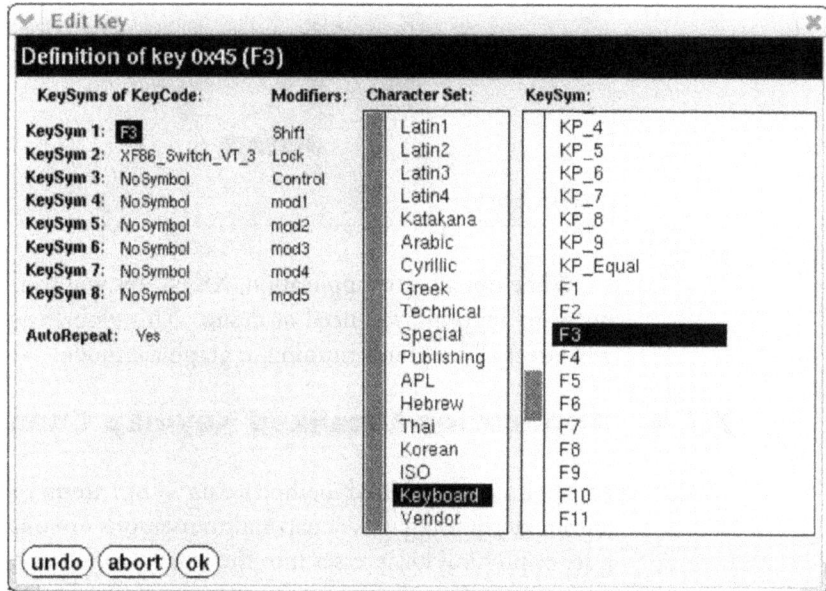

```
# Select the KeySym associated with the modifier in question,
in this case the modifier will be Control for the control key
and for F3 this is KeySym F3. Select a character set and then
the appropriate KeySym. Repeat for all appropriate keys.
```

Figure 7.2 shows the dialog box for editing the key definition for F13.

```
# Select Write Output button
```

Figure 7.3 shows the message box displaying your write output.

```
# From command line or part of a startup script run 'xmodmap
.xmodmap-`uname -n` to invoke your keyboard change.
```

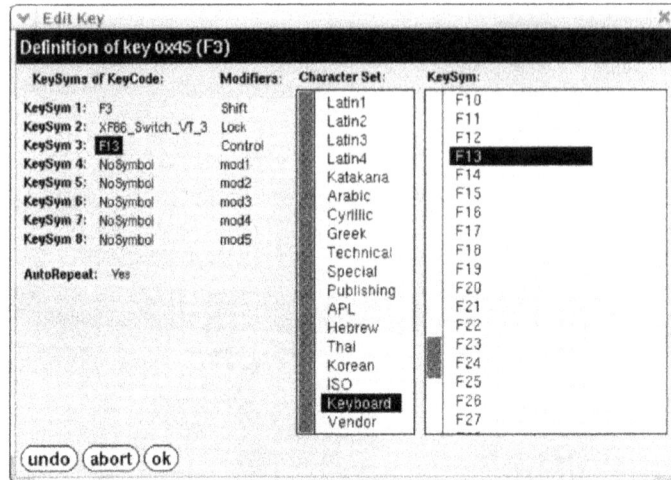

While not a pretty application, XKeyCaps will work to remap your keyboard to anything you need or desire. This global change to your keymap will affect all programs running in graphical mode.

7.1.4   Application Localized Keymap Change

An application-localized method exists within xterm to remap the keys only within xterm using its keymap and translations options. xterm will translate a set of physical key presses into the entry of another key sequence into the text stream. A script that performs the mapping for you allows the creation of a new command, vmsterm, to connect to a VMS machine with the proper keymap without affecting any other running programs. This method is preferred and is fully discussed on the xterm FAQ (http://dickey.his.com/xterm/xterm.faq.html), where scripts different from the following are also presented. However, you should note some similarities, since there are only a few ways to perform this mapping process. This script will map the keys shown in Table 7.1.

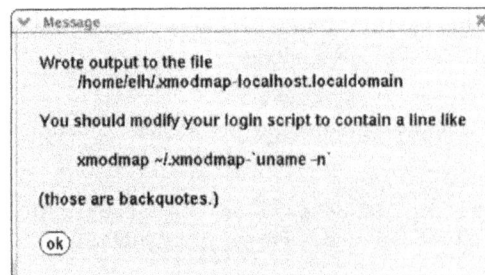

Table 7.1   *Key Mapping Script*

Key	Map
Shift F3	F13
Shift F4	F14
Shift F5	F15 (Help)
Shift F6	F16 (Do)
Shift F7	F17
Shift F8	F18
Shift F9	F19
Shift F10	F20
Shift F11	F11
Shift F12	F12
Print	Help (F15)
Cancel	Do (F16)
Pause	Keypad Minus
Insert	Insert Here
Delete	Remove
Home	Find
End	Select
Prior	Prev
Next	Next
BackSpace	BackSpace (sends DEL - ascii 127)
Num_Lock	PF1
KP_Divide	PF2
KP_Multiply	PF3
KP_Subtract	PF4
KP_Add	Keypad Comma
KP_Enter	Enter
KP_Decimal	Period
KP_0	Keypad 0
KP_1	Keypad 1

Table 7.1   *Key Mapping Script (continued)*

Key	Map
KP_2	Keypad 2
KP_3	Keypad 3
KP_4	Keypad 4
KP_5	Keypad 5
KP_6	Keypad 6
KP_7	Keypad 7
KP_8	Keypad 8
KP_9	Keypad 9

VMSTERM

```
#!/bin/sh
xterm -title "VMSTERM" -sb -geometry 80x24 -xrm \
'XTerm*VT100.Translations: #override \n \
    Shift  <Key>F3:         string(0x1b)  string("[25~") \n \
    Shift  <Key>F4:         string(0x1b)  string("[26~") \n \
    Shift  <Key>F5:         string(0x1b)  string("[27~") \n \
    Shift  <Key>F6:         string(0x1b)  string("[28~") \n \
    Shift  <Key>F7:         string(0x1b)  string("[29~") \n \
    Shift  <Key>F8:         string(0x1b)  string("[31~") \n \
    Shift  <Key>F9:         string(0x1b)  string("[32~") \n \
    Shift  <Key>F10:        string(0x1b)  string("[33~") \n \
           <Key>Print:      string(0x1b)  string("[28~") \n \
           <Key>Cancel:     string(0x1b)  string("[29~") \n \
           <Key>Pause:      string(0x1b)  string("Om") \n \
           <Key>Insert:     string(0x1b)  string("[2~") \n \
           <Key>Delete:     string(0x1b)  string("[3~") \n \
           <Key>Home:       string(0x1b)  string("[1~") \n \
           <Key>End:        string(0x1b)  string("[4~") \n \
           <Key>Prior:      string(0x1b)  string("[5~") \n \
           <Key>Next:       string(0x1b)  string("[6~") \n \
           <Key>BackSpace:  string(0x7f)  \n \
           <Key>Num_Lock:   string(0x1b)  string("OP") \n \
           <Key>KP_Divide:  string(0x1b)  string("OQ") \n \
           <Key>KP_Multiply: string(0x1b) string("OR") \n \
           <Key>KP_Subtract: string(0x1b) string("OS") \n \
           <Key>KP_Add:     string(0x1b)  string("Ol") \n \
           <Key>KP_Enter:   string(0x1b)  string("OM") \n \
           <Key>KP_Decimal: string(0x1b)  string("On") \n \
```

```
         <Key>KP_0:        string(0x1b)   string("Op") \n \
         <Key>KP_1:        string(0x1b)   string("Oq") \n \
         <Key>KP_2:        string(0x1b)   string("Or") \n \
         <Key>KP_3:        string(0x1b)   string("Os") \n \
         <Key>KP_4:        string(0x1b)   string("Ot") \n \
         <Key>KP_5:        string(0x1b)   string("Ou") \n \
         <Key>KP_6:        string(0x1b)   string("Ov") \n \
         <Key>KP_7:        string(0x1b)   string("Ow") \n \
         <Key>KP_8:        string(0x1b)   string("Ox") \n \
         <Key>KP_9:        string(0x1b)   string("Oy") \n \' \
-e /usr/bin/telnet $1
```

7.1.5   Other Tools

In addition to the aforementioned terminal tools, there is a for-fee tool available on Windows and Linux. PowerTerm, an $89 product, will provide terminal access using many different terminal formats with the proper keyboard maps or tools to access the proper keyboards. PowerTerm (http://www.ericom.com/pti.asp) will emulate a tn3270 and VT52 through VT525 terminals, as well as many others.   PowerTerm's major advantage, other than support for many different terminal types in one program, is its ability to display the proper keyboard for the terminal type necessary, as shown in Figure 7.4. This displayed keyboard will allow you to use the appropriate keys for your application with the click of the mouse and not require the modification of the global keymap or specialized scripts for localized modifications.

7.2   How Do I Access Windows Terminal Services?

More and more programs are moving from the mainframe to Windows systems. To access these programs, Linux needs a method to communicate with the Terminal software on the Windows box. To do this, Linux can make use of the rdesktop (http://www.rdesktop.org) tool, which already ships on many versions of Linux. However, rdesktop only displays an 8-bit 800x600 window by default. To use a different bit depth, you will need to upgrade rdesktop to version 1.3.1—for example, for a 24-bit 1,280 × 1,024 desktop using v1.3.1:

```
rdesktop —a 24 —geometry 1280x1024 hostname
```

Figure 7.4
*Keyboard mapping
with PowerTerm.*

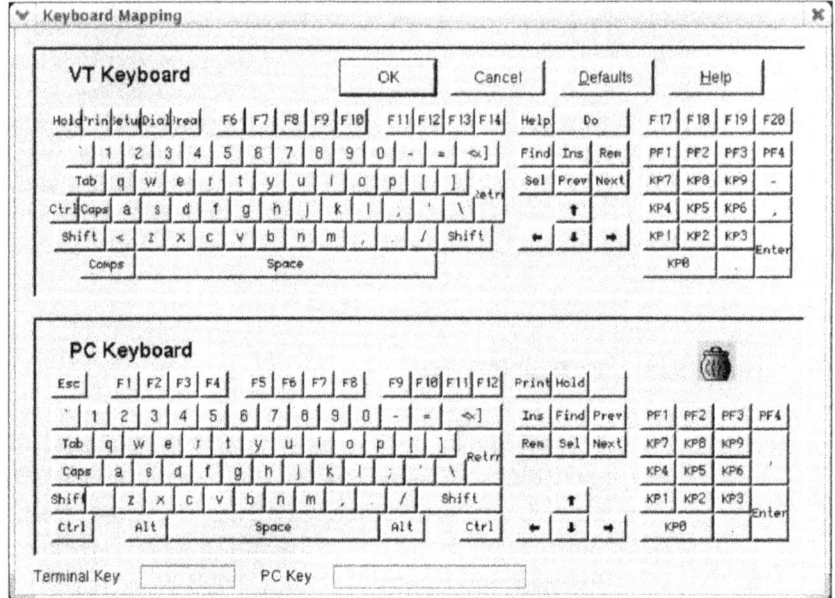

7.2.1   RHEL3 8-bit Version

```
up2date rdesktop
```

7.2.2   v1.3.1 for Systems without This Version

```
tar -xzf rdesktop-1.3.1.tgz
cd rdesktop-1.3.1
./configure
make
make install
```

Mandrake/SLES9/RHEL4/Fedora

Already part of the operating system.

When using rdesktop, a login box similar to ones presented when you are sitting at the Windows machine will be presented (see Figure 7.5). Since each rdesktop command in use will start a new login session there is no method to use rdesktop as a session sharing tool, however once logged in all the normal desktop sharing tools are available to you. rdesktop does not get around the need for a Terminal Server license for its connections as the Terminal Server is running on your Microsoft Windows platform.

Figure 7.5
New rdesktop login screen.

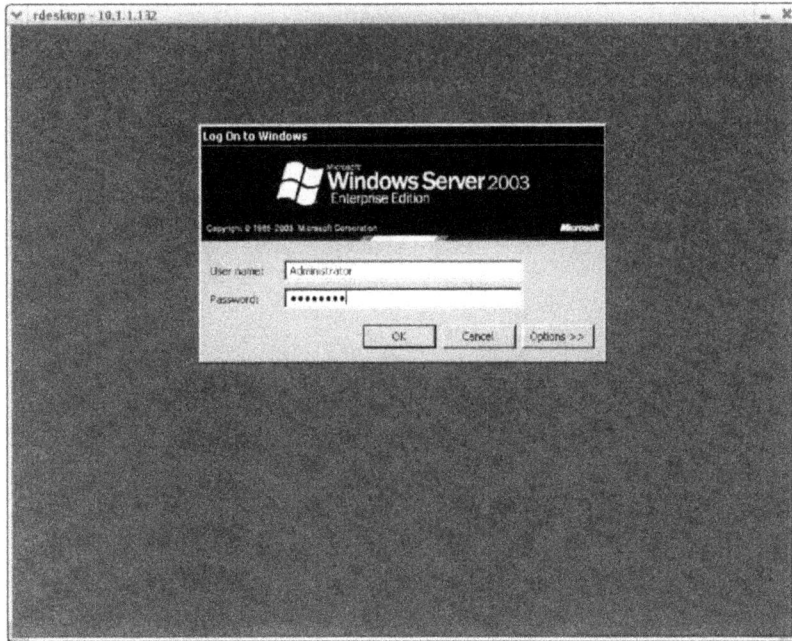

7.3   How Do I Access Citrix Metaframe Server?

Citrix Metaframe servers are very easy to access using the free Metaframe client from Citrix. This client can be found at http://www.citrix.com and behaves in the same way as it does on Windows. If the client is integrated into an existing distribution (as it is with RHEL3), it can be accessed from the system menus.

7.3.1   RHEL

```
up2date ICAClient
```

Startup is from the *Red Fedora->Internet->Citrix ICA Client* menu item. On first startup, you will need to agree to the license agreement. Once the license is agreed to, then the client can be used in exactly the same way as it is used on Windows. Figure 7.6 shows the first Citrix window.

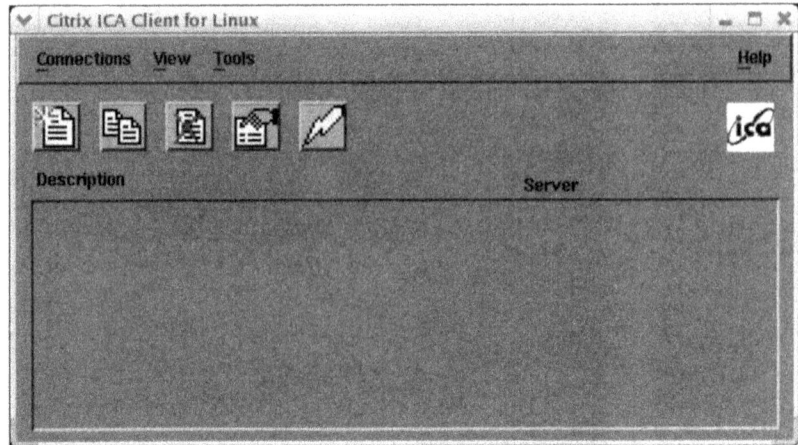

Figure 7.6
*Citrix Metaframe
server.*

7.4   The Cost

Terminal server clients offer interesting licensing concerns, when using rdesktop for example, you will still need a Terminal Server license for the client to be able to connect, the same holds true for the Citrix Metaframe client. With Citrix, this is in addition to the Citrix Metaframe license. On Windows, use of Citrix does not require the addtional Terminal Server license however. So use of these tools could be slightly more expensive than other options.

Other than using a tool like PowerTerm there are no other costs associated with the presented clients.

7.5   Support

Support exists for PowerTerm and Citrix from each vendor. For xterm, support is through the Linux distribution vendor, for a 3270 emulator, support varies based on which client is in use.

The costs are displayed in Table 7.2.

Table 7.2   *Cost of Linux Replacements for Terminal Services Clients*

Software	Support Level	Fee	Support Fee
VMware	Web-based/Phone	$199	Free for 90 days and you would still need to purchase a terminal emulator
Xterm	Through Linux vendor, if at all	NA	NA
PowerTerm	Web-based/Phone	$89	15% of the final purchase price for one year
ICAClient	Phone	For server only. You will need a certificate for Citrix to use. If using from Linux, you will also need a certificate for Terminal Services.	For server only
tn3270	varies	varies	varies

8

Home Office Tools

This chapter will discuss tools that are more commonly found on the home desktop but can be found on the corporate desktop as well. We will show solutions for connecting Palm or Pocket PC handheld devices to the Linux desktop and discuss mechanisms to synchronize your PDA's data. Specifically, we will look at synchronizing photographs and Documents-To-Go files with the PDA. In addition, we review accounting programs and digital camera solutions.

8.1   How Do I Synchronize My PDA with Linux?

Synchronizing your Palm OS device with Linux is quite simple if you have pilot support for your desktop, mail client, and pilot-link installed. Most, if not all, of these are available directly from each distribution; however, they are not always installed. There are several subsets to this question we will also address. It should be noted that newer Palm devices might require a change to the visor kernel module to work properly (This modification is generally to the visor.h file in your kernel source directory. Refer to the http://www.pilot-link.org website for updates for your kernel visor module.) While this change is relatively trivial, it can void warranties on Enterprise Linux distributions. At the very least, the following programs are needed to synchronize a Palm device with Linux.

8.1.1   RHEL

```
up2date pilot-link
up2date gnome-pilot
up2date evolution
```

Pilot-link provides the basic tools to synchronize your Palm device with Linux, while the others add more features to the system, including automatic synchronization when the Palm device is connected (gnome-pilot), a conduit settings editor (gnome-pilot), and the ability to synchronize your Palm calendar, notes, and addresses (Novell Evolution). With all three tools, synchronizing your Palm device with Linux becomes very straight-forward. However, finding the proper port is not always simple, and for that you will need to use the pilot-link tools directly. There are, however, some general rules; the first is that Visor devices use /dev/ttyUSB0 and Palm devices use /dev/ttyUSB1, so try those in the appropriate order. These devices are not always accurate, and for Sony devices they could be reversed. It also should be noted that the USB port does not correspond to the physical USB device.

8.1.2   Finding the Proper Port for Your Palm

The dlpsh command will allow you to print out information about your Palm device. This information can be used to verify connectivity as well as providing a handy command line interface to gain information about the files stored on you palm. When the device asks you to press the HotSync button, do so and you will be connected only if you chose the proper device. Since I am synchronizing a Palm Tungsten device, I chose to use /dev/ttyUSB1 first, and it connected after HotSync was started. Some-times you need to press HotSync before running dlpsh. Try both meth-ods. I then issue the df command to read data from the Palm device and verify its accuracy against the Palm device. It should be noted that there are also serial port connections available to dlpsh. The devices in question will be /dev/ttyS0 or /dev/ttyS1, depending on which device the Palm cradle is plugged into.

```
dlpsh —p /dev/ttyUSB1
   Listening to port: /dev/ttyUSB1

   Please press the HotSync button now... Connected



Welcome to the DLP Shell
Type 'help' for additional information

dlpsh> df
Filesystem          1k-blocks       Used    Available     Used      Total
Card0:ROM           16515072         n/a     16515072      n/a      16128k
Card0:RAM           66060288    39247176     26813112      59%      64512k
Total (ROM + RAM)   82575360    55762248          n/a      n/a     80640k9
```

Figure 8.1
*Configuration tool
for gnome-pilot.*

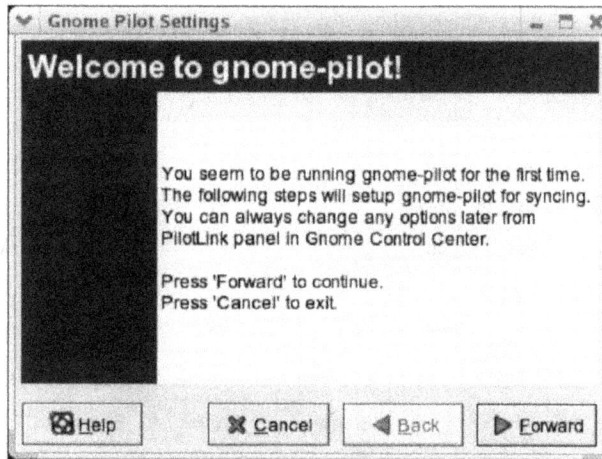

Now that the Palm port is known, in this case /dev/ttyUSB1, we use this to configure the automatic synchronization tool, gnome-pilot. Select *Red Fedora->Preferences->More Preferences->PalmOS Devices* to launch the gnome-pilot applet (gpilotd-control-applet) to start the gnome-pilot configuration tool (Figure 8.1).

Then press *Forward* to select the USB port for your Palm (Figure 8.2).

Be sure to select /dev/ttyUSB1 or, if you are only going to synchronize this Palm device to your system, you can make a symbolic link to /dev/pilot to simplify matters.

```
ln -s /dev/ttyUSB1 /dev/pilot
```

Once the proper port, speed, and USB selection are made, continue selecting *Forward*. Where a selection on whether this is the first time the Palm Device has been synchronized to this machine is presented (Figure 8.3), select *Yes* and then *Forward*.

Now it is time to perform your first HotSync so that the gnome-pilot software can retrieve the Palm UserName and Palm ID from the Palm device. If this dialog box appears, I always select *Yes*. The only time *No* would be selected is if the Palm device had never been initialized with a username or never been synchronized from or to any other HotSync software. The HotSync dialog box is shown in Figure 8.4.

If for some reason the Palm device does not synchronize, verify the permissions of the port used. In this case, /dev/ttyUSB1 had permissions of rw-rw---- (ls -al /dev/ttyUSB1) and ownership of root.uucp,

Figure 8.2
Cradle settings for
Palm in gnome-
pilot.

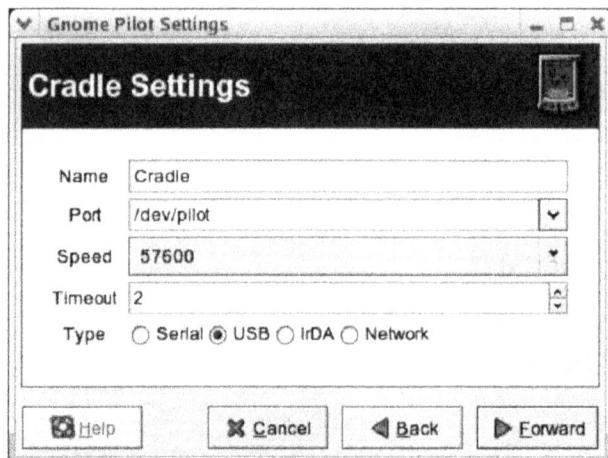

Figure 8.3
Pilot identification
dialog box for
gnome-pilot.

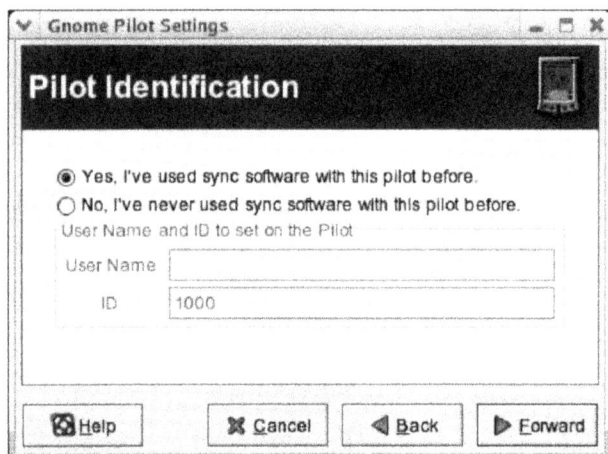

which implies that only root and those users in the uucp group can access the device. You will need to correct this before you can proceed; once the permissions are fixed, the gpilotd process must to be killed so it can restart with the proper permissions. It should be noted that on a standard (non-hardened) installation modification of the /etc/security/console.perms file to include /dev/ttyUSB0 and /dev/tyUSB1 to the pilot definition line is all that is needed to allow access to the device. After making this change you will need to logout and log back in. Once access to the USB device is granted, the synchronization can proceed. The resulting dialog box from a successful synchronization is shown in Figure 8.5.

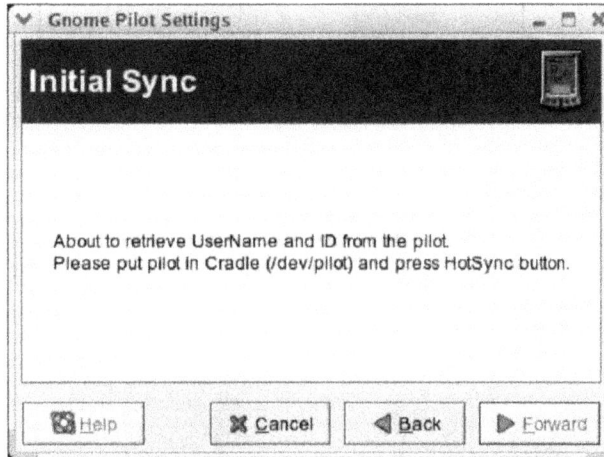

Figure 8.4
The first HotSync via gnome-pilot.

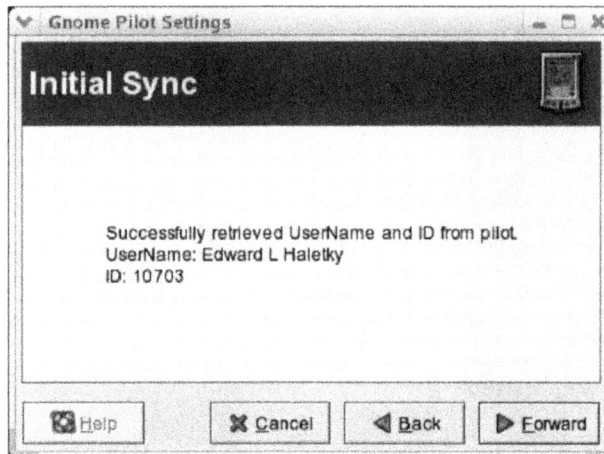

Figure 8.5
Successful initial synchronization.

Select *Forward* to continue to select the Pilot File repository and name of the Palm device for purposes of using gnome-pilot to synchronize multiple devices (Figure 8.6).

Once *Forward* is selected, the configuration of the gnome-pilot synchronization software is complete (Figure 8.7), and the next time the HotSync button is pressed, automatic synchronization will occur between the Palm device and Linux. All that is left is to configure all the conduits to perform as desired.

Select *Apply* to proceed to the section on configuring the appropriate conduits (Figure 8.8).

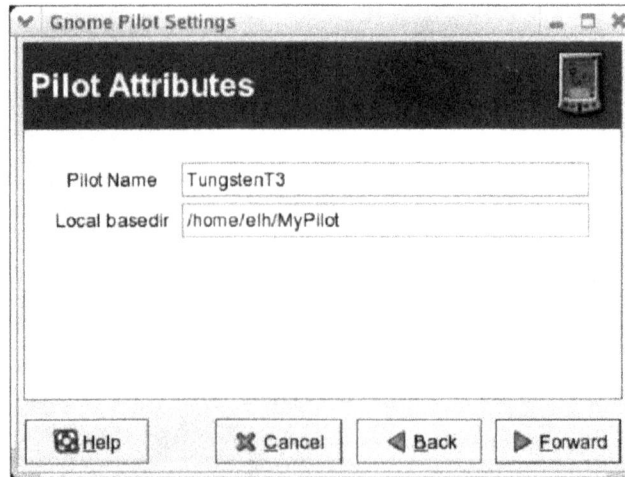

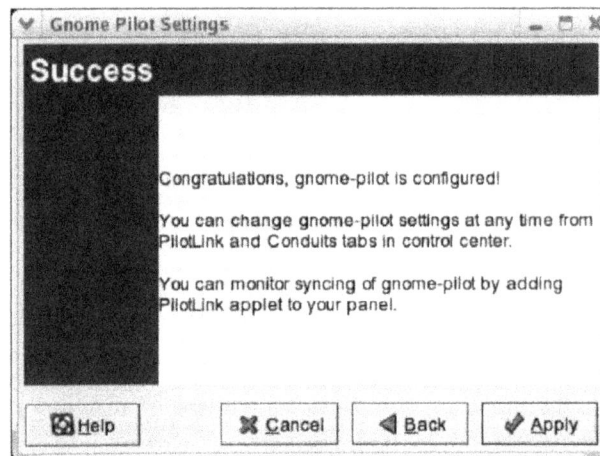

The *Conduits* tab will show all loaded conduits for configuration (Figure 8.9). These loaded conduits can be configured easily from this interface to perform as desired. For the first time it is recommended that the conduits be enabled and set to *Synchronize* with a one-time action of *Copy from Pilot*.

Enabling *Backup* will copy all files from the Palm Main memory to the appropriate location (Figure 8.10). However, the major failing of the Palm software for Linux is that it will not synchronize to any Secure Digital, Memory Stick, or MMC Card memory. For this it is recommended that you use a card reader/writer.

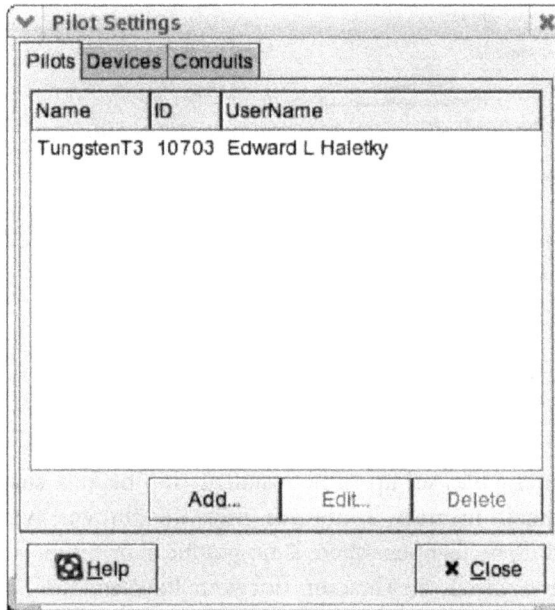

Figure 8.8
Configuring pilot settings via gnome-pilot.

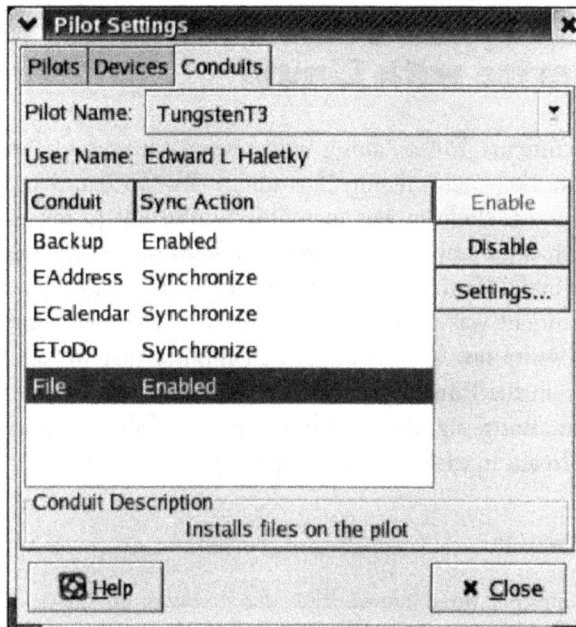

Figure 8.9
Configuring conduits in gnome-pilot.

Now the all-important first synchronization is ready. The Palm will synchronize its Address, Calendar, and ToDo lists with Evolution, as well as

Figure 8.10
*Setting up the
backup for the first
synchronization.*

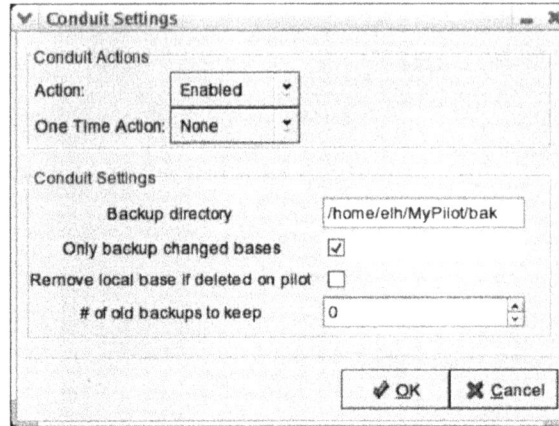

install any files set up to be installed, and make a complete backup of the Palm main memory. To do this, press the HotSync button on the Palm. As the HotSync happens there is no graphical or progress bar shown. You can, however, check the directory for your Pilot and see if it is filled with data; also, of course, you could monitor the Palm device itself.

8.2   How Do I Synchronize Documents to Go on My Palm Device with Linux?

Documents-To-Go, along with several Linux tools, was used to write this book. So synchronizing Documents-To-Go data from the Palm device to the Linux desktop was incredibly important to me. Doing this is actually much easier now than it was when I first started working on the research for this book. Until Documents-To-Go 6 was released, the internal format of a document was proprietary to DataViz. Now, Documents-To-Go can read and write raw Word files, which implies that we can just place the .doc files on the Palm device and not be concerned about translation. This simplifies things significantly; however, it was almost impossible prior to release 6. To aid in this, the following script could be used:

```
#!/bin/sh
##
# Convert Word/Excel file to Documents to Go 6.0 Format
# And prepare for sync
##

##
# Word Files
```

```
##
doc="MSWD"
typ="DTGP"
name=`basename $1 .doc`
if [ $name = "$1" ]; then name=`basename $1 .DOC`; doc="MSWD";
fi
##
# Excel Files
##
if [ $name = "$1" ]; then name=`basename $1 .xls`; doc="MSXL";
fi
if [ $name = "$1" ]; then name=`basename $1 .XLS`; doc="MSXL";
fi
##
# Pictures?
##
if [ $name = "$1" ]; then name=`basename $1 .jpg`; doc="Foto";
typ="Foto"; fi
if [ $name = "$1" ]; then name=`basename $1 .JPG`; doc="Foto";
typ="Foto"; fi

##
# Convert to Docs to Go stream Format
##
if [ $name != "$1" ]
then
    par c -a "stream" $name.pdb $name $doc $typ $1
    pilot-xfer -i $name.pdb
else
    echo "$0: error: $1 is not a Word or Excel file"
fi
```

The script uses the par tool (http://www.djw.org/product/palm/par/), which is easily installed and used to convert files to the appropriate streamed data mode. This simple conversion will allow Microsoft Word, Excel, and Photos to be synchronized to the Palm device's main memory using the pilot-xfer command which requires the palm to be connected and ready for a hotsync in order to be used. pilot-xfer is not a delayed write to the palm but immediate. As of Documents To Go v7.0 PowerPoint documents can be edited in their native format on the Palm. This will require that the script be amended with the following lines to be placed above the Pictures comment to handle the new format.

```
if [ $name = "$1" ]; then name=`basename $1 .ppt`; doc="MSPT";
if [ $name = "$1" ]; then name=`basename $1 .PPT`; doc="MSPT";
```

To build par:

```
tar —xzf prc.tgz
cd prc
make
make install
```

8.3   How Do I Synchronize Pictures to My Palm from Linux?

See the previous section, since the provided script will also convert `.jpg` files to the appropriate format. First convert all possible picture formats to the JPEG format and run the script with the file to transfer as the only argument.

8.4   Is There a Microsoft Money or Quicken Equivalent?

There are several Microsoft Money or Quicken equivalents; however, none of them will edit the Microsoft Money or Quicken databases directly. You can, however, export to the appropriate file format, and Linux-based tools such as GnuCash (http://www.gnucash.com), KMyMoney, and others will read the file formats. It may be better to completely switch to one or the other; however, this may not be possible if your account or tax software will not work without a proper Money or Quicken database. In this case, Cross-Over Office may be your solution of choice. I use GnuCash to manage my accounts and do not need to worry about tax software or an accountant, since the reports are sufficient for those needs.

GnuCash will track stock portfolios, as well as various bank accounts and other assets and expenses. This tool may not be as pretty as the commercial tools, but it will work to track your accounts and provide accurate data. However, GnuCash is difficult to install if it is not native with your version of Linux, because you may need packages that do not exist except in a future revision of the OS.

8.4.1   Mandrake

Part of install.

8.4.2   SuSE

Part of install.

8.4.3   Red Hat Versions before 3

```
up2date gnucash
```

8.4.4   RHEL3

```
Download from Fedora site (http://fedora.redhat.com)
bonobo-1.0.22-8.1.src.rpm
gal-0.24-3.1.src.rpm
GConf-1.0.9-13.1.src.rpm
gnome-print-0.37-9.src.rpm
gnome-vfs-1.0.5-18.src.rpm
gnucash-1.8.9-1.src.rpm
gtkhtml-1.1.9-8.src.rpm
Guppi-0.40.3-18.src.rpm
g-wrap-1.3.4-5.1.src.rpm
libghttp-1.0.9-9.1.1.src.rpm
libofx-0.6.6-1.src.rpm
oaf-0.6.10-9.1.src.rpm
openhbci-0.9.14-2.src.rpm
docbook-dtds-1.0-24.src.rpm
docbook-style-dsssl-1.78-3.src.rpm
openjade-1.3.2-11.1.src.rpm

Download from your RHEL3 RHN website (http://www.redhat.com)
guile-1.6.4-8.src.rpm

# rpmbuild --rebuild guile-1.6.4-8.src.rpm
# rpm -Uvh --force /usr/src/redhat/RPMS/i386/{guile-1.6.4-
8.i386.rpm,guile-devel-1.6.4-8.i386.rpm}
# rpmbuild --rebuild oaf-0.6.10-9.1.src.rpm
# rpm -ivh /usr/src/redhat/RPMS/i386/{oaf-0.6.10-
9.1.i386.rpm,oaf-devel-0.6.10-9.1.i386.rpm}
# rpmbuild --rebuild gnome-print-0.37-9.src.rpm
# rpm -ivh /usr/src/redhat/RPMS/i386/{gnome-print-0.37-
9.i386.rpm,libgnomeprint15-0.37-9.i386.rpm,gnome-print-devel-
0.37-9.i386.rpm}
# rpmbuild --rebuild bonobo-1.0.22-8.1.src.rpm
# rpm -ivh /usr/src/redhat/RPMS/i386/{bonobo-1.0.22-8.1.
i386.rpm,bonobo-devel-1.0.22-8.1.i386.rpm}
# rpmbuild --rebuild GConf-1.0.9-13.1.src.rpm
```

```
# rpm -ivh /usr/src/redhat/RPMS/i386/{GConf-1.0.9-13.1.i
386.rpm,GConf-devel-1.0.9-13.1.i386.rpm}
# rpmbuild --rebuild gnome-vfs-1.0.5-18.src.rpm
# rpm -ivh /usr/src/redhat/RPMS/i386/{gnome-vfs-1.0.5-1
8.i386.rpm,gnome-vfs-devel-1.0.5-18.i386.rpm}
# rpmbuild --rebuild gal-0.24-3.1.src.rpm
# rpm -ivh /usr/src/redhat/RPMS/i386/{gal-0.24-
3.1.i386.rpm,gal-devel-0.24-3.1.i386.rpm,libgal23-0.24-
3.1.i386.rpm}
# rpmbuild --rebuild libghttp-1.0.9-9.1.1.src.rpm
# rpm -Uvh /usr/src/redhat/RPMS/i386/{libghttp-1.0.9-
9.1.1.i386.rpm,libghttp-devel-1.0.9-9.1.1.i386.rpm}
# rpmbuild --rebuild gtkhtml-1.1.9-8.src.rpm
# rpm -ivh /usr/src/redhat/RPMS/i386/{gtkhtml-1.1.9-8.i3
86.rpm,gtkhtml-devel-1.1.9-8.i386.rpm}
# rpmbuild --rebuild Guppi-0.40.3-18.src.rpm
# rpm -ivh /usr/src/redhat/RPMS/i386/{Guppi-0.40.3-18.i3
86.rpm,Guppi-devel-0.40.3-18.i386.rpm}
# rpmbuild --rebuild g-wrap-1.3.4-5.1.src.rpm
# rpm -ivh /usr/src/redhat/RPMS/i386/{g-wrap-1.3.4-5.1.i
386.rpm,g-wrap-devel-1.3.4-5.1.i386.rpm}
# rpmbuild --rebuild openhbci-0.9.14-2.src.rpm
# rpm -ivh /usr/src/redhat/RPMS/i386/{openhbci-0.9.14-
2.i386.rpm,openhbci-devel-0.9.14-2.i386.rpm}
# rpmbuild --rebuild docbook-dtds-1.0-24.src.rpm
# rpmbuild --rebuild openjade-1.3.2-11.1.src.rpm
# rpmbuild --rebuild docbook-style-dsssl-1.78-3.src.rpm
# rpm -Uvh /usr/src/redhat/RPMS/i386/{openjade-1.3.2-
11.1.i386.rpm,openjade-devel-1.3.2-11.1.i386.rpm} /usr/src/
redhat/RPMS/noarch/docb{docboook-dtds-1.0-24.0-
24.noarch,docbook-style-dsssl-1.78-3.noarch.rpm}
# rpmbuild --rebuild ofx-0.6.6-1.src.rpm
# rpm -ivh /usr/src/redhat/RPMS/i386/{libofx-0.6.6-
1.i386.rpm,libofx-devel-0.6.6-1.i386.rpm}
# rpmbuild --rebuild gnucash-1.8.9-1.src.rpm
# rpm -ivh /usr/src/redhat/RPMS/i386/{gnucash-1.8.9-
1.i386.rpm,gnucash-backend-postgres-1.8.9-1.i386.rpm}
# perl -MCPAN -e shell
cpan> install Finance::Quote
cpan> install Finance::QuoteHist
cpan> install Date::Manip
cpan> quit
```

Installation of these packages should not adversely affect RHEL3. However, if a problem does arise, you will have to remove the packages for testing, since RHEL3 has a standard set of packages and additions must sometimes be removed before progressing with any form of debug.

Gnucash provides a very good help file to go over the import of Microsoft Money and Quicken files into itself using QIF or OFX file formats.

8.5 Is There a QuickBooks Equivalent?

GnuCash (http://www.gnucash.org) will work as a business tool but does not import or read Quickbooks files. However, if you are using CrossOver Office, you can use QuickBooks Pro with no issues. Please note that you will need version 4 of CrossOver Office for QuickBooks to run properly in CrossOver Office. Installation of QuickBooks follows all the normal instal-

Figure 8.11
Welcome window for QuickBooks in CrossOver Office.

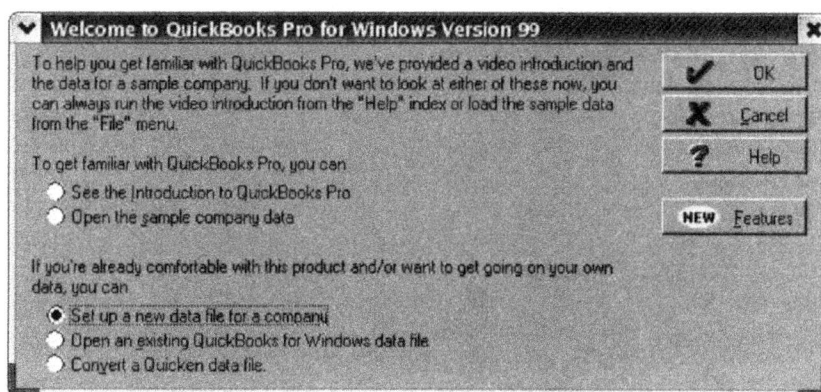

lations inside CrossOver. Once the installation is complete, launching and running is done as normal (Figure 8.11). Even the upgrade process for QuickBooks works seamlessly.

Since many accountants require a professional package such as QuickBooks, there is no equivalent to the real thing.

8.6 How Do I Download Pictures from My Digital Camera?

I use a Canon PowerShot A70 and Canon EOS 20D. Since the default install of gPhoto2 does not support the EOS 20D, an upgrade is required. GPhoto2 version 2.1.5 is required per the documentation at http://www.gphoto.org. To verify that everything works as you expect, you can run the following commands from a shell; included is the expected example output (Figure 8.12).

```
$ gphoto2 --auto-detect
Model                         Port
-----------------------------------------------------------
Canon PowerShot A70           usb:
Canon PowerShot A70           usb:004,029
$ gphoto2 --shell
gphoto2: {/home/xxx/laptop/camera} /> cd store_00010001
Remote directory now '/store_00010001'.
gphoto2: {/home/xxx/laptop/camera} /store_00010001> ls
DCIM/              MISC/
gphoto2: {/home/xxx/laptop/camera} /store_00010001> cd DCIM
Remote directory now '/store_00010001/DCIM'.
gphoto2: {/home/xxx/laptop/camera} /store_00010001/DCIM> ls
464CANON/
gphoto2: {/home/xxx/laptop/camera} /store_00010001/DCIM> cd 464CANON
Remote directory now '/store_00010001/DCIM/464CANON'.
gphoto2: {/home/xxx/laptop/camera} /store_00010001/DCIM/464CANON> ls
IMG_6460.JPG        IMG_6462.JPG        IMG_6463.JPG        IMG_6464.JPG
IMG_6465.JPG        IMG_6466.JPG        IMG_6467.JPG        IMG_6468.JPG
IMG_6469.JPG        IMG_6470.JPG        IMG_6471.JPG        IMG_6472.JPG
IMG_6473.JPG        IMG_6474.JPG        IMG_6475.JPG        IMG_6476.JPG
IMG_6477.JPG        IMG_6478.JPG        IMG_6479.JPG        IMG_6480.JPG
IMG_6481.JPG        IMG_6482.JPG        IMG_6483.JPG        IMG_6484.JPG
IMG_6485.JPG        IMG_6486.JPG
```

8.6.1 RHEL3

When upgrading the gtkam and gphoto2 packages on RHEL3, a copy of libexif is required, and the gtkam-gimp package will not be upgraded. As a result, gimp camera picture acquire functionality is lost.

```
# rpmbuild --rebuild libexif-0.5.12-3.src.rpm #(From Fedora
Core 3 or other repository)
# rpm -ivh /usr/src/redhat/RPMS/i386/{libexif-0.5.12-
3.rpm,libexif-devel-0.5.12-3.rpm}
# tar -xzf libgphoto2-2.1.5.tar.gz
# cd libgphoto2-2.1.5
# edit packaging/rpm/package.spec.in and comment out the lines
@RPM_LIBUSB_DEVEL_TRUE@Requires: libusb >= 0.1.8
@RPM_LIBUSB_DEVEL_TRUE@BuildRequires: libusb-devel >= 0.1.8
# ./configure --prefix=/usr
# make rpm
# cp /etc/hotplug/usb.usermap /etc/hotplug/usb.usermap.orig
# rpm -Uvh --force --nodeps packaging/rpm/RPMS/i386/*.rpm
# /usr/lib/libgphoto2/print-usb-usermap > /etc/hotplug/
usb.usermap
```

```
# cp packaging/linux-hotplug/usbcam.console /etc/hotplug/usb/
usbcam
# cd ..
# tar -xzf gphoto2-2.1.5.tar.gz
# cd gphoto2-2.1.5
# ./configure --prefix=/usr
# make
# cd packgeing/rpm
# edit Makefile and change rpm -define to be rpmbuild -define.
# make rpm
# rpm -Uvh RPMS/i386/gphoto2-2.1.5-1.i386.rpm
# cd ../../..
# tar -xzf gtkam-0.1.12.tar.gz
# cd gtkam-0.1.12
# ./configure --prefix=/usr
# edit packaging/rpm/Makefile and change rpm -define to be
rpmbuild -define
# edit the file packaging/rpm/package.spec and comment out the
following lines:
%files gimp
%defattr(-,root,root)
%{_libexecdir}/gtkam-gimp
# edit the file packaging/rpm/package.spec and remove the word
MANUAL from the line:
%doc README COPYING AUTHORS NEWS MANUAL
# make rpm
# rpm -Uvh --nodeps packaging/rpm/RPMS/i386/gtkam-0.1.12-
1.i386.rpm
```

While rebuilding gphoto2 and gtkam is NOT for the faint of heart, you should gain access to the latest version that supports the latest cameras. Also, since gtkam uses gphoto commands you will not necessarily need to upgrade the gtkam software but you will need to upgrade gphoto2. This version is what I need to use, since the standard RHEL3 package does not support the latest cameras. It recognizes the Canon EOS 20D, but it will not communicate very well with it; however, it handles the Canon Power-Shot A70 with ease. A firmware bug prevents the Canon EOS 20D from working properly. In this case, we will need to upgrade the camera before using gphoto2/gtkam, as well as upgrade the software to 2.1.6 when it's released, since this will provide a workaround to the firmware issue.

Even if you do not plug the camera directly into the machine, there are always USB card readers that work flawlessly. They are treated just like hard drives.

Figure 8.12
*gtkam picture
download from
camera.*

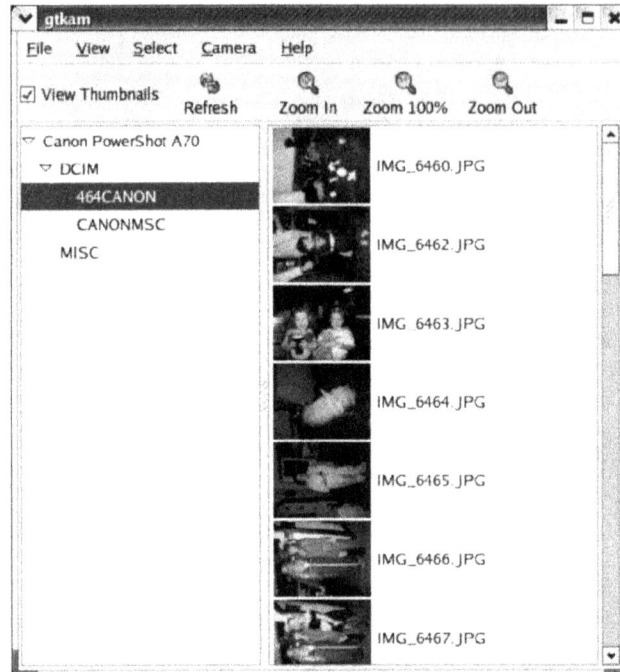

8.7   How Do I Sync my iPAQ with Linux?

The iPAQ device can also be used with Linux but the integration with tools like Evolution is not as complete as it requires revisions of software that is not currently in the mainstream of use. While the synce-multisync_plugin package will integrate the synce package into the desktop and Evolution, the installation instructions are very sparse and the procedures did not provide a successful sync. The manual use of synce does however provide a means to sync an iPAQ on Linux. This section was not written by the Author, but Pat Lampert, a colleague who owns an iPAQ.

If you wish to use a Windows CE device such as an iPaq Pocket PC with Linux you will need to install SynCe. SynCe is a set of open source tools available from SourceForge.net at the following web site:

```
<http://synce.sourceforge.net/synce/index.php>
```

As of the writing of this book the most current version of Synce is 9.0-1. An rpm for this software along with optional rpms can be downloaded from the site. The basic steps for using Synce are as follows:

1. Install SynCE on your Linux machine

2. Configure SynCE

3. Establish a connection (aka synch) with your Windows CE device

4. Use the tools provided to copy files to and from the device, and perform other operations.

5. Disconnect your WinCE device.

Of course steps 1 and 2 are one-time only events.

My tests were performed using a Compaq 3700 series iPaq Pocket PC. As you will find on the Synce web site there are special steps you may need to take depending on the device you are using. In my case it was quite straightforward.

8.7.1 Installation of Synce

You will see from the web site that Synce has other kits available for synchronizing your address book and other options. For this book I am keeping it simple, and just downloading the software needed to establish a synch. The software needed for a simple connection with your Windows CE device which consists of a single rpm package: synce-0.9.0-1.i386.rpm.

Install synce-0.9.0-1.i386.rpm using the rpm command:

```
# rpm -Uvh synce-0.9.0-1.i386.rpm
Preparing...
######################################## [100%]
```

8.7.2 Synce Configuration

Once Synce is installed then you need to configure Synce. The installation instructions vary depending on the type of Windows CE device you are using, the version of Linux, and what type of port you are using. More details on available on the Source Forge Synce web site.

In my case, as I mentioned earlier, I had an iPaq with a USB connector. Because I was using a usb connector I had to follow some special instructions and use modprobe to enable the iPaq usb serial module.

The following three commands must be performed by the root user.

```
$ /sbin/modprobe ipaq
```

The next step is to configure Synce to use the proper port for connection. This is done with the synce-serial-config command. In my case I was connecting to USB port 0 so the command needed was:

```
# synce-serial-config ttyUSB0
```

After the port is identified then the command to start up the daemon that detects connections is:

```
# synce-serial-start
synce-serial-start is now waiting for your device to connect
```
This can be added to your system startup if needed.

Next you need to set up any user that will be synching with your device to run dccm. This command must be run from the user account. This command can be added to the user's .login file if wanted.

```
$ dccm
```

Once the above steps have been performed you should be able to start a manual synch using the Windows CE Active Synch icon on your Pocket PC.

If you have difficulties, especially with a USB connection. The following Source Forge Synce web page is very helpful.

```
<http://synce.sourceforge.net/synce/usb_linux.php>
```

Also examine or tail the file /var/log/messages for errors from the synce-serial-start and dccm commands.

8.7.3   Synce Tools

After you have successfully established a synch connection between your Windows CE device and your Linux desktop there are a variety of command line tools available to perform various operations with your device.

pstatus

Allows you to obtain status on your connection and information about the device you have connected.

Example:

```
$ pstatus
Version
=======
Version:      3.0.11171 (Merlin: Pocket PC 2002)
Platform:     3 (Windows CE)
Details:      " "

System
======
Processor architecture: 5 (ARM)
Processor type:         2577 (StrongARM)
Page size:              0x10000

Power
=====
ACLineStatus: 01 (Online)

Status for main battery
=========================
Flag:            1 (High)
LifePercent:     100%
LifeTime:        Unknown
FullLifeTime:    Unknown

Status for backup battery
=========================
Flag:            1 (High)
LifePercent:     100%
LifeTime:        Unknown
FullLifeTime:    Unknown

Store
=====
Store size: 48922624 bytes (46 megabytes)
Free space: 15883432 bytes (15 megabytes)

Memory for storage: 49061888 bytes (46 megabytes)
Memory for RAM:     17145856 bytes (16 megabytes)
```

pls

allows you to obtain a listing of the files on your Windows CE device

```
$ pls
Archive              315  Tue 04 Jan 2005 08:33:45 PM EST
BatmanBeginsMovi56k.asxArchive      849  Tue 04 Jan 2005
08:32:12 PM EST  EnjoythisLiveper0k.asx
```

```
Archive              898  Sun 01 Feb 2004 09:48:44 PM EST
Playlist.asx
Archive           970420  Sun 08 Jun 2003 10:28:56 AM EDT
Recording1.wav
Archive           109631  Thu 22 Nov 2001 08:00:48 PM EST  Learn
More.pdf
Archive           399120  Fri 16 Nov 2001 08:00:26 PM EST  Acrobat
Reader User Guide.pdf
Directory                 Tue 20 Aug 2002 10:14:18 PM EDT
Annotations/
Directory                 Mon 03 Sep 2001 08:00:01 AM EDT
Business/
Directory                 Mon 03 Sep 2001 08:00:01 AM EDT
Personal/
Directory                 Mon 03 Sep 2001 08:00:00 AM EDT
Templates/
```

pmkdir

Will create a directory (or folder) on your WinCE device. In the example below a folder named patrick is created on the windows CE device from your Linux desktop and then I use pls to list the files and folders on the windows CE device.

```
$ pmkdir patrick
$ pls
Directory                 Wed 05 Jan 2005 08:34:13 PM EST
patrick/
Archive              315  Tue 04 Jan 2005 08:33:45 PM EST
BatmanBeginsMovi56k.asxArchive        849  Tue 04 Jan 2005
08:32:12 PM EST  EnjoythisLiveper0k.asx
Archive              898  Sun 01 Feb 2004 09:48:44 PM EST
Playlist.asx
.
.
```

pcp

This command is used to copy files to and from the Windows CE device

The following example copies a file named myfile.txt to the windows CE device. Note that the file name on the Windows CE device must be in quotes and preceeded with a colon. The colon is used by pcp to determine which argument signifies the Windows CE device.

```
$ pcp myfile.txt ":myfile.txt"
```

To copy a file off the Windows CE device to your Linux machine use this command:

```
$ pcp ":myfile.txt" fromPDA.txt
```

prm removes a file from the Windows CE device. Note that no special formatting is required for the prm command.

First lets see whats on the PDA.

```
$ pls
Directory               Wed 05 Jan 2005 08:34:13 PM EST
patrick/
Archive             315 Tue 04 Jan 2005 08:33:45 PM EST
BatmanBeginsMovi56k.asx
.
.

$ prm myfile.txt
```

prmdir will remove a directory

```
$ prmdir patrick
```

Now observe that the Batman movie and patrick are gone...

```
$ pls
Archive             849 Tue 04 Jan 2005 08:32:12 PM EST
EnjoythisLiveper0k.asx
Archive             898 Sun 01 Feb 2004 09:48:44 PM EST
Playlist.asx
Archive          970420 Sun 08 Jun 2003 10:28:56 AM EDT
Recording1.wav
.
.
```

Other commands available are prun to run a program on the Windows CE device from your Linux machine, and synce-install-cab to install a .cab file.

After you have completed your work, simply remove the device from its cradle or connector and the synch will disconnect.

8.8   The Cost

While these relatively esoteric tools are not commonplace they are being used more and more in the normal business world. Quickbooks, especially, is the tool of choice for many small businesses; many people need digital cameras for support and work purposes, and Palm type devices are becoming commonplace in the environment. The cost of using these tools and external devices are not as high as you may expect. There are native versions of many tools or if necessary the relatively inexpensive CrossOver Office tool to gain access to tools like QuickBooks, or even the more expensive VMware.

8.9   Support

The major support concern is the availability of software for the myriad of devices that can be attached to the USB slots on your computer. This ranges from your Palm, iPaq to a Camera. Support for the OpenSource projects is active and excellent.

8.10   Conclusion

The learning curve may be higher when using native tools, yet they will greatly expand your Linux desktop experience. Add in Wine and even more external devices can be attached and used effectively.

The costs of the software necessary to use these tools are displayed in Table 8.1.

Table 8.1   *Cost of Linux Replacements for Terminal Service Clients*

Software	Support Level	Fee	Support Fee
CrossOver Office	Web-based/Phone	$69	Free for 90 days
GnuCash	Web-based/e-mail	NA	NA
Evolution	Web-based/e-mail	NA	NA
gnome-pilot	Web-based/e-mail	NA	NA
gphoto2/gtkam	Web -based/e-mail	NA	NA
Pilot-link	Web-based/e-mail	NA	NA

Virus and Spam Protection

The two worst enemies of the desktop are spam and viruses. These two villains cause all administrators major frustration. The good thing about using a Linux desktop is that there are very few Linux viruses; however, spam is still a villain! A number of tools can combat these two ruffians for Linux; there are key configurations that will help to secure your system from viruses. The most common method of virus infiltration is via e-mail, so this chapter will concentrate on making e-mail safer for Linux machines.

9.1   How Do You Stop Spam?

Spam, we can all admit, is a major pain. To combat spam, there are several tools available for a Linux box; these tools can be implemented at the user level or system-wide. Some tools will learn from messages marked spam, and others require manual control. One of the most widely used tools is SpamAssassin. SpamAssassin combines all the features and learning control into one highly configurable package. The tool will allow you to use remote services as well as its own rules for determining whether an e-mail is spam, and the user can configure it globally as well, using the procmail subsystem of sendmail and other mailers. Since sendmail is the most common mailer, we will look into its use.

If an IMAP server running SpamAssassin is in use, otherwise Spam-Assassin will have no effect on exchange mail via this combination of tools. SpamAssassin is designed to work as part of the system mailer via the procmail subsystem, which is used for the local delivery of email at a user basis, or using other mechanisms can be a system level mail filter (milter). If mail is delivered local to the server the milter can find SPAM before some other transfer mechanism is invoked, including POPmail and IMAP. Therefore SpamAssassin can be used for Outlook clients that get their email via an IMAP or POPmail server. SpamAssassin has the added advantage of being shipped as a part of many versions of Linux. To use SpamAssassin for locally delivered e-mail, you can use procmail, as follows:

Create *.forward* file:

```
"|IFS=' ' && exec /usr/bin/procmail —f - || exit 75 #user"
```

Create *.procmailrc* file:

```
:0fw: spamassassin.lock
* < 256000
| spamassassin
```

With these instructions entered the local sendmail delivery agent will run spamassassin or spamc (server-based) program and tag all your e-mail as spam or ham (not spam, but good e-mail or ham). Since, in some cases, legitimate e-mail is incorrectly marked as spam, it may be better to not redirect all spam to other mailboxes. You can add the following commands to the *.procmailrc* file to forward all spam mail to other folders so you are not bothered with them. However, this behavior is probably best left up to your mail client.

```
:0:
* ^X-Spam-Level: \*\*\*\*\*\*\*\*\*\*
spam—folder

:0:
* ^X-Spam-Status: Yes
possible-spam-folder
```

These additional *.procmailrc* file entries will look at SpamAssassin headers. All items with a score of 10 or more will be marked as spam and placed in the spam-folder directly or the possible-spam-folder if the mail could be considered spam.

With procmail in use, you can formulate a recipe to handle just about every case of spam. SpamBouncer (http://www.spambouncer.org) does just that; however, this tool does not contain the powerful Bayesian filter that is a part of SpamAssassin.

If you are using an e-mail client such as Evolution, or your mail is not delivered locally, you may need another method to protect against spam. The following set of instructions assumes that your remote mail server does

Figure 9.1
*Adding a
SpamAssassin filter
to Evolution: filters
dialog box.*

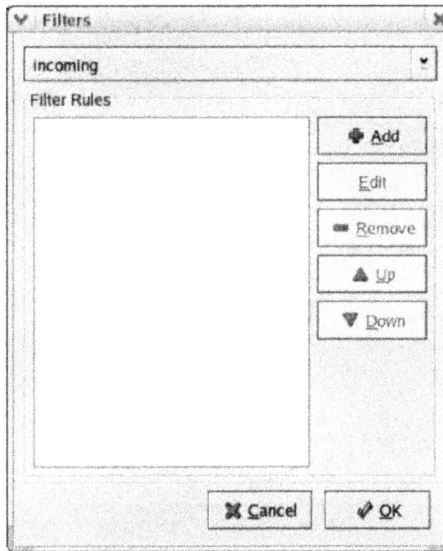

not already have a tool to block spam or that you wish to augment this
facility.

Adding SpamAssassin filter to Evolution:

Navigate to *Tools->Filters...* (Figure 9.1).

Click on *Add*, then change the *Rule* name to *SpamAssassin* and in the *If*
clause change the condition to *Pipe Message to Shell Command*. Enter *spamassassin –e > /dev/null* in the box next to the condition. Select *returns greater
than* from the *Returns* drop-down box, and enter *0* as the value to *return
greater than*. (See Figure 9.2.)

Now modify the *Then* clause of the filter and select *click here to select a
folder* and either add a new folder or select an existing spam Folder. In this
example, we use a folder named spam that resides in the *Local Folders* folder
(see Figure 9.3). Add a secondary condition to *Stop processing*; if you do not
do this, other filters will still run on the spam mail. Be sure this rule is the
first rule in your *Filter* list.

If your mail server already tags spam, instead of calling a shell command,
you can look for a specific mail header (perhaps the Subject header as Spam-
Assassin can change the subject to be proceeded with the tag *** SPAM ***)
and perform the same Move to Folder actions to capture spam. In addition to
installing SpamAssassin, you will want to install the tools to talk to outside
servers. These outside servers look at Black Lists (RBL) as well as member

Figure 9.2
Adding a
SpamAssassin filter
to Evolution:
adding
SpamAssassin.

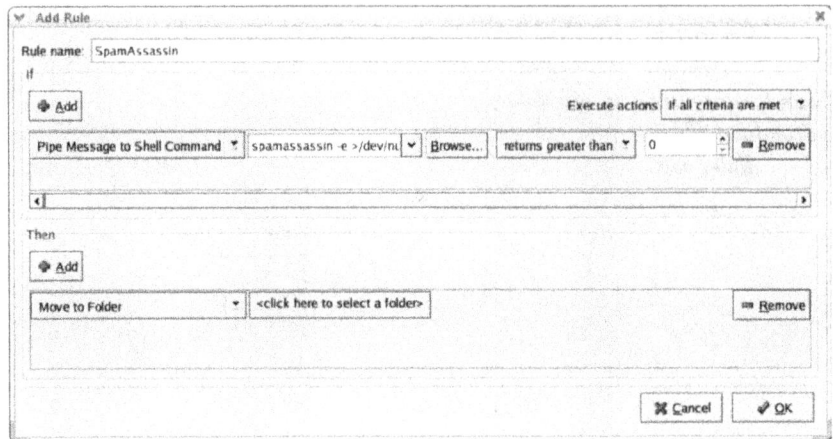

Figure 9.3
Adding a
SpamAssassin filter
to Evolution: add
a folder for spam.

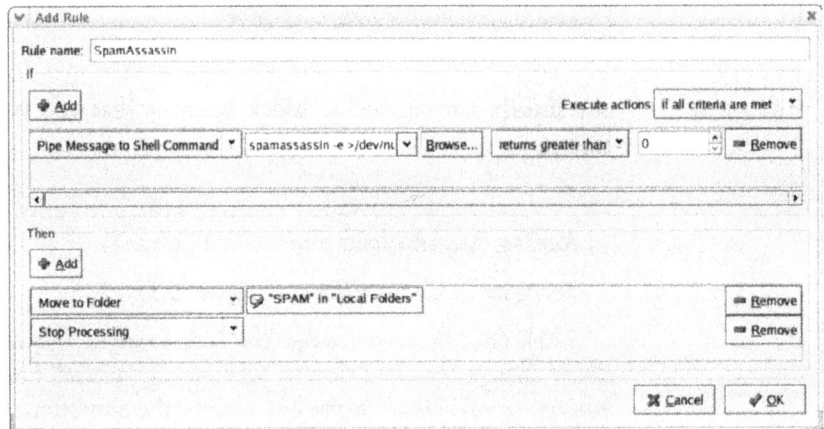

votes, to determine if an e-mail footprint is considered spam. There are three such external tools: Pyzor, Razor, and DCC.

9.1.1   RHEL3

```
up2date spamassassin
```

For a mail server, it may be better to implement something system- or network-wide instead of the individual approach documented here. For that you will need to integrate SpamAssassin into your mail server software.

9.2   How Can You Stop Spam and E-mail Viruses?

The MailScanner (http://www.sng.ecs.soton.ac.uk/mailscanner/) tool can stop spam and e-mail viruses. MailScanner is a series of scripts and tools that will integrate with your existing Mail Transport Agent. This system-/ network-wide tool will process each e-mail through SpamAssassin as well as through its own virus and spam filters. MailScanner also integrates with many different antivirus tools for Linux. While its install is not trivial, the install script will handle everything for you.

```
# tar —xzf MailScanner-4.36.4-1.rpm.tar.gz
# cd MailScanner-4.36.4-1
# ./install.sh
```

Once the software is installed, we need to configure the software to use SpamAssassin as well as your virus scanner. While MailScanner contains a very basic virus scanner, it does not contain something that will by default catch all known viruses; to accomplish this, you will need a better virus scanner.

9.2.1   Enabling SpamAssassin Support in MailScanner

Edit */etc/MailScanner/MailScanner.conf* and verify that the line *Spam Checks = yes* is set. If, instead, it reads *Spam Checks = no*, enable this feature. Next, change the line *Use SpamAssassin = no* to *Use SpamAssassin = yes*. This will enable the use of SpamAssassin via the SpamAssassin Perl interface.

There is also a */etc/MailScanner/spam.assassin.prefs.conf* file you can edit to set your SpamAssassin configuration. Three spam detection and filtering networks can be added to SpamAssassin to block even more spam. They are Vipul's Razor, Pyzor, and DCC.

- Vipul's Razor (http://razor.sourceforge.net/)

- Pyzor (http://pyzor.sourceforge.net)

- DCC (http://www.rhyolite.com)

Installation of Pyzor, Razor, and DCC will greatly increase the effectiveness of SpamAssassin, since these tools interact with network-wide servers to determine and grade e-mail footprints based on RBL, black-hole lists, and voting systems. A detailed discussion of the installation and configuration of these tools is outside the scope of this book. If Razor and Pyzor are installed then their perl or python interfaces will be used by the SpamAssassin rules, however, DCC will require the path to be entered into /etc/MailScanner/spam.assassin.prefs.conf as a line reading

```
dcc_path /usr/local/bin/dccproc
```

Which will allow SpamAssassin to find the third tool to block spam.

Last, you can create central *spam* and *nospam* mailboxes that will update the Bayesian database with new spam or ham entries when a user wants that to happen. You can use the following shell script every hour or so:

```
#!/bin/sh
/usr/bin/sa-learn —spam —mbox —no-rebuild /var/spool/mail/spam
/usr/bin/sa-learn —ham —mbox —no-rebuild /var/spool/mail/nospam
/usr/bin/sa-learn —rebuild
```

Rebuilding the Bayesian database after all the spam and ham are found will speed up the processing of each mailbox. Granted, you can add appropriate aliases into your mail subsystem as well; however, if you have a lot of e-mail being reported as spam, you may only want to process it every so often instead of immediately.

9.2.2   Enabling Antivirus Support

MailScanner supports many different virus scanners; one product is free, but the other products must be purchased before you can use any of the virus definitions. These definitions will include all known definitions for windows and Linux. Currently, the list includes the following (the Cost column includes both mail-filtering and file system–scanning versions of the software).

Product	Web Site	Cost
Sophos	http://www.sophos.com	$$$$
McAfee	http://www.mcafee.com	$
Command	http://www.command.co.uk	$$
Kaspersky	http://www.kaspersky.com	$$$

NOD32	http://www.nod32.com	$$
F-Secure	http://www.f-secure.com	$
F-Prot	http://www.f-prot.com	$$$
Panda	http://www.pandasoftware.com	$$
RAV	http://www.ravantivirus.com	$$
AntiVir	http://www.antivir.de	$$$
ClamAV	http://www.clamav.net	—
Trend	http://www.trendmicro.com	$$$

To select the appropriate software for MailScanner, you would edit the file */etc/MailScanner/MailScanner.conf* and verify that the line *Virus scanning = yes* is set. If instead it reads *Virus scanning = no*, enable this feature. Next, change the line *Virus Scanners =* to be *Virus Scanners = clamav*. This will enable the use of ClamAV as the virus scanner of choice. Since ClamAV is an active project with active virus updates, it is an inexpensive option to use. Sophos is available, but it is quite expensive to use. However, picking a virus scanner is corporate policy, and MailScanner can support all the scanners mentioned. Last, you can use more than one scanner on the definition line. If you wanted, you could use all the scanners listed by adding one at a time in a space-separated list.

ClamAV is quite easy to install:

```
# tar —xzf clamav-0.80.tar.gz
# cd clamav-0.80
# useradd —d /var/clamav clamav
# ./configure
# make
# make install
```

Once ClamAV is installed, let MailScanner handle the rest. To speed up mail filtering you can install the ClamAV Perl module; there is also a Perl module for Sophos. These Perl modules interact with a central virus-scanning server. Instructions for installing Perl modules are on the MailScanner Web site.

9.3   How Can You Scan a Machine for Viruses?

In the same way that you use ClamAV to scan for e-mail viruses, you can use it to scan a disk for viruses. The key is to keep the virus software up-to-date, and ClamAV provides freshclam to do just that. By default, freshclam runs daily. Clamscan, ClamAV's antivirus scanner, does not run daily or at all in an automated fashion. You can set up clamscan to be run by each user individually or via the whole system. I like the complete system approach, since it centralizes control. To this end, creating the file */etc/cron.daily/doclamscan* will run the antivirus file system scanner daily, and the output will automatically be e-mailed to root, so that the administrator can handle any problems:

```
#!/bin/sh

/usr/bin/clamscan --stdout -r --exclude /files --exclude /mnt /
> /var/log/clamscan.log
grep -v "OK$" /var/log/clamscan.log | grep -v "Excluded" | grep
-v "Empty file\.$"
```

Clamscan can take as many *--exclude* options as you wish to give it. In our case, we are ignoring external file systems, which will greatly speed up the processing. The output would be similar to the following in root's e-mail.

```
/etc/cron.daily/doclamscan:

LibClamAV Warning: Multipart MIME message contains no boundaries
LibClamAV Warning: messageFindArgument: no '=' sign found in MIME header
LibClamAV Warning: Multipart MIME message contains no boundaries
LibClamAV Warning: Unsupported multipart format `knowbot' - report to
bugs@clamav.net
LibClamAV Warning: Descriptor[12]: Bad format or broken data
//usr/share/doc/clamav-0.80/test/clam-error.rar: RAR module failure
//usr/share/doc/clamav-0.80/test/clam.exe.bz2: ClamAV-Test-File FOUND
//usr/share/doc/clamav-0.80/test/clam.cab: ClamAV-Test-File FOUND
//usr/share/doc/clamav-0.80/test/clam.exe: ClamAV-Test-File FOUND
//usr/share/doc/clamav-0.80/test/clam.rar: ClamAV-Test-File FOUND
//usr/share/doc/clamav-0.80/test/clam.zip: ClamAV-Test-File FOUND
//usr/share/doc/clamd-0.80/clamdwatch/clamdwatch.tar.gz: Eicar-Test-Signature
FOUND
//home/xxx/laptop/mail/clamav-0.80/test/clam-error.rar: RAR module failure
//home/xxx/laptop/mail/clamav-0.80/test/clam.cab: ClamAV-Test-File FOUND
//home/xxx/laptop/mail/clamav-0.80/test/clam.exe: ClamAV-Test-File FOUND
//home/xxx/laptop/mail/clamav-0.80/test/clam.rar: ClamAV-Test-File FOUND
```

```
//home/xxx/laptop/mail/clamav-0.80/test/clam.zip: ClamAV-Test-File FOUND
//home/xxx/laptop/mail/clamav-0.80/test/clam.exe.bz2: ClamAV-Test-File FOUND
//home/xxx/laptop/mail/clamav-0.80/contrib/clamdwatch/clamdwatch.tar.gz: Eicar-
Test-Signature FOUND
//home/xxx/xxxxxx/xxxxxxxxxxxxxxxxxxxxxxxx/564d1449-3bae-cf98-993e-
e4fb727f7a85.vmem: Exploit.HTML.MHT-1 FOUND
//home/xxx/xxxxxx/xxxxxxxxxxxxxxxxxxxxxxxx/xxxxxxxxxxxxxxxxxxxxxx-000001-
s002.vmdk: Exploit.HTML.MHT-1 FOUND

----------- SCAN SUMMARY -----------
Known viruses: 28956
Scanned directories: 54578
Scanned files: 295985
Infected files: 14
Data scanned: 44633.56 MB
I/O buffer size: 131072 bytes
Time: 11523.822 sec (192 m 3 s)
```

As can be seen from the output, several viruses have been found in various file formats. Only two of them are a concern, since the others are issues caused by test files in the ClamAV install. You can safely remove such test files. RAR failures imply that the RAR module is not working or the RAR archive is corrupt, so we would need to look into these issues. These are just some hints for interpreting the report. If the last line of the doclamscan script was not there, then the email for a virus scan would report on every file on the system and the output would be extremely difficult to interpret.

9.4 The Cost

Everyone can agree that the cost of NOT protecting your system from SPAM and virus' will be much more than NOT protecting your system and thereby the network. However, this does not imply that the most expensive solution is the best for your corporation. For virus filtering, many of the existing corporate definitions can be used, or the inexpensive tools or even active developed free tools.

9.5 Support

Support for each of the tools must be considered as these are evils that must be conquered. MailScanner and SpamAssassin are very actively developed tools, while SpamBouncer is infrequently updated. There is even purchasable Support for MailScanner from third parties that will augment the distribution support that may be available for SpamAssassin. The cost of support from these companies varies greatly. In addition, clamav while an active opensource project may not be what is required when major virus companies are providing milters of their own for Linux based mail transport agents.

9.6 Conclusion

Pick which tools are required by your IT department or if going it alone, use MailScanner with SpamAssassin and ClamAV to get a full implementation of SPAM and Virus checking. The various software packages discussed in this chapter are displayed in Table 9.1.

Table 9.1 *Cost of Linux-compatible Antivirus and Antispam Software*

Software	Support Level	Fee	Support Fee
MailScanner	Mailing List or commercial	NA	Depends on vendor
SpamAssassin	Mailing List or commercial	NA	Depends on vendor
ClamAV	Mailing List or commercial	NA	Depends on vendor
SpamBouncer	Mailing List	NA	NA

10

Training Tools

There is a wide range of tools that people use on the corporate desktop for online training. The most basic tool would be the Web browser, with all the Plug-ins available while the more complex tool will be a proprietary set of programs and CD-ROMS. This chapter will review both sets of tools with the idea of running training on the Linux desktop.

Since there is an awful lot of training material available, we cannot cover it all within a single chapter, we will subset this to more of the training-enabling tools and those programs available for training someone to take the Cisco Certified Network Administrator (CCNA) exam.

Training-enabling tools could be standalone tools such as NetMeeting, media players, and specialized plug-ins for Web browsers. Since most training tools are designed to run on Microsoft Windows, finding those that work under Linux is difficult. Some companies, such as Mindleaders, Inc. (http://www.mindleaders.com), have tools for just about all operating systems available, while other companies target Windows. In this chapter, we will be looking at this extremely small list of computer/Web–based training tools:

WebEx (http://www.webex.com)

NetMeeting (http://www.microsoft.com/netmeeting)

LiveMeeting (http://www.microsoft.com/livemeeting)

CCNA Complete (http://www.cisco.com)

Cisco CCNA Network Simulator (http://www.cisco.com)

Sybex CCNAGold virtual router lab software (http://www.sybex.com)

10.1   How Can I Use WebEx on Linux?

There is no native WebEx client for Linux; however, when using Internet Explorer via CrossOver Office, you can download and successfully use the WebEx client and Player. Access to WebEx is extremely simple. Proceed to the http://www.webex.com Web site and download the client per the Web pages from an Internet Explorer window running within Wine.

While WebEx can be used as a playback tool, it also has a method to provide direct access to live feeds, much like NetMeeting can.

You will need to first sign into WebEx in order to use the tool (Figure 10.1).

Figure 10.1
Logging into WebEx.

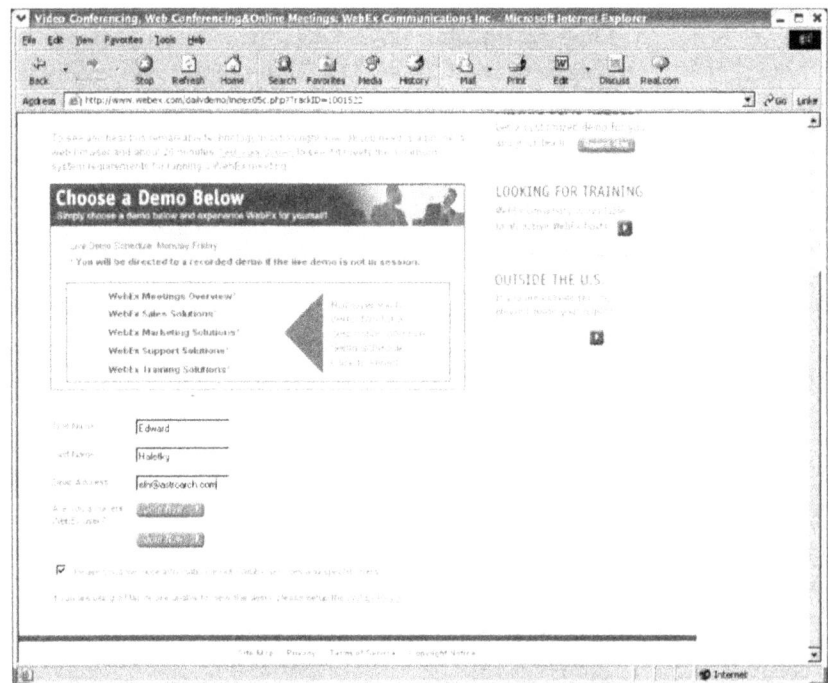

Once you sign in, you will be presented with a dialog to download and run the WebEx client (Figure 10.2).

And, finally, your WebEx player will run so that the presentation will display and allow you control over the media (Figure 10.3).

Without Wine, WebEx is not usable. With Wine, the player works just as you would expect and provides the necessary tool to enable a meeting or view a course.

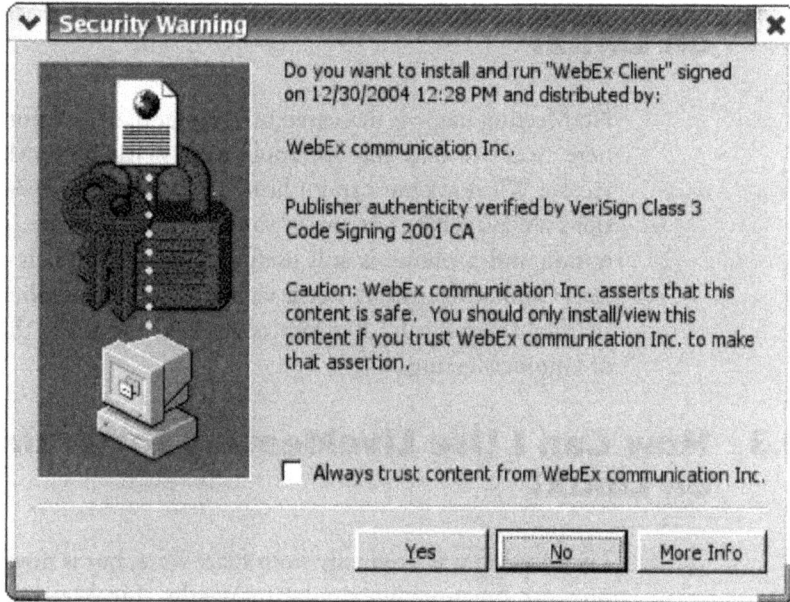

Figure 10.2
Installing WebEx Client.

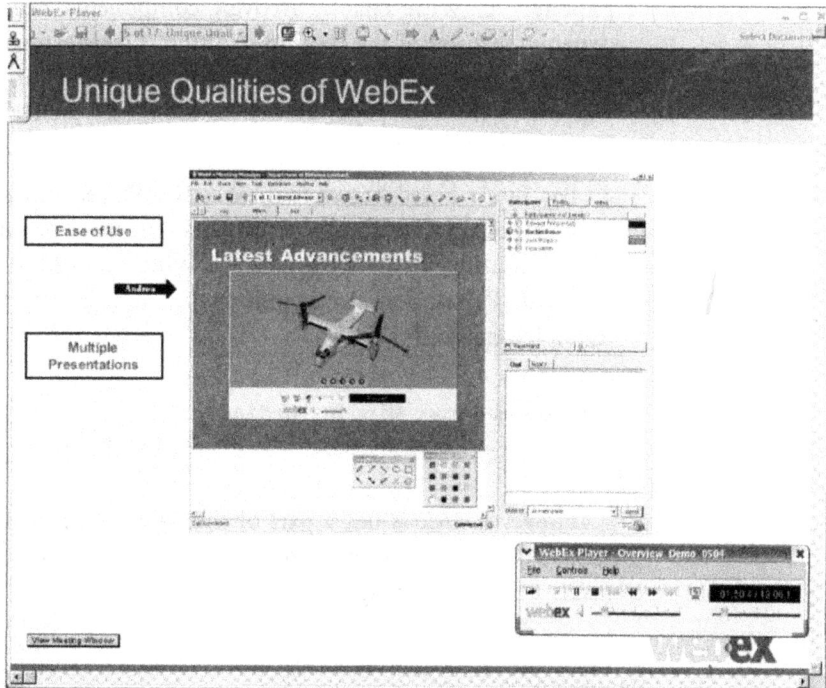

Figure 10.3
Running WebEx Client.

10.2   How Can I Use NetMeeting for Training on Linux?

NetMeeting usage is discussed in Chapter 6, so will not be covered in depth here except to state that for application sharing, NetMeeting on Linux can receive Windows but cannot host any sharing. However, all the other functions are available. The use of sound via the network is not always a viable option and a phone is still useful to have around. It should be reiterated that GnomeMeeting is not a viable option for application or whiteboard sharing, since the T.120 protocol necessary to make this work is not a part of GnomeMeeting.

10.3   How Can I Use LiveMeeting for Training on Linux?

LiveMeeting was originally from PlaceWare, but is now from Microsoft and provides functionality similar to WebEx. LiveMeeting claims it can work with any browser. For playback, however, when using Mozilla or Firefox, LiveMeeting displays static windows and must go to a blank page to listen to any sound, so always open sound into a new window. The use of Internet Explorer via Wine enables ActiveX components necessary for the more dynamic features of the tool. In addition, LiveMeeting will present data to be replayed in RealPlayer, MediaPlayer, and WAV formats. In addition, it will use static Web pages as well as Flash and ActiveX aspects of a Web browser to display its content.

For Linux-based browsers there is RealPlayer, mplayer, xine, and Flash plug-ins to handle each of the contents, but those based on ActiveX can be displayed using Internet Explorer via Wine. In order to use xine to display the MediaPlayer, x-ms-wmx, mime type, we will need to add the following to /etc/pluggerrc-5.1.3:

```
video/x-ms-wmx: Windows Media
exits nokill: xine —pq "$file" 2>/dev/null 1>/dev/null
```

However, xine is not a part of the base install; it is available at http://xinehq.de/ and is installed via the standard download and build mechanisms per the following:

```
tar —xzf xine-lib-1.0.tar.gz
cd xine-lib
```

```
./configure
make
make install
cd ..
tar —xzf xine-ui-0.99.3.tar.gz
cd xine-ui
./configure
make
make install
```

10.4 How Does One Take Computer-Based CCNA Training?

Cisco Certified Network Associate (CCNA) Training is provided by many methods including, computer based methods (CBT). Of the computer based methods we have reviewed, there are three tools for use with Linux. While none of them has Linux alternatives, some of them are available via Wine, and others only via tools such as VMWare.

All these CBT methods work in VMWare, while some work under Wine.

10.4.1 CCNA Complete V1.0

While CCNA Complete does not run on Linux, it will run under CodeWeavers Wine. In order to get this to happen you must first copy the file C:\Windows\WINHLP32.EXE from a Windows 98 or Windows 2000 (Windows XP may also work; however, I have not tried this) machine to <location of your Wine Bottle>/Windows directory and ensure the permissions are set to execute for everyone, as follows:

```
cp WINHLP32.EXE ~/.cxoffice/dotwine/fake_windows/Windows
chmod 755 ~/.cxoffice/dotwine/fake_windows/Windows/
WINHLP32.EXE
```

As long as there is a winhlp32.exe executable in the proper location, everything will work as you would expect. The install is handled through the Wine install tools, and you can then select from the Red Fedora Menu for the CCNA Complete Course Navigator (Figure 10.4).

When running the program, the Begin Reading button will launch the winhlp32.exe application with its reading material (Figure 10.5).

Figure 10.4
*CCNA Complete
Course Navigator.*

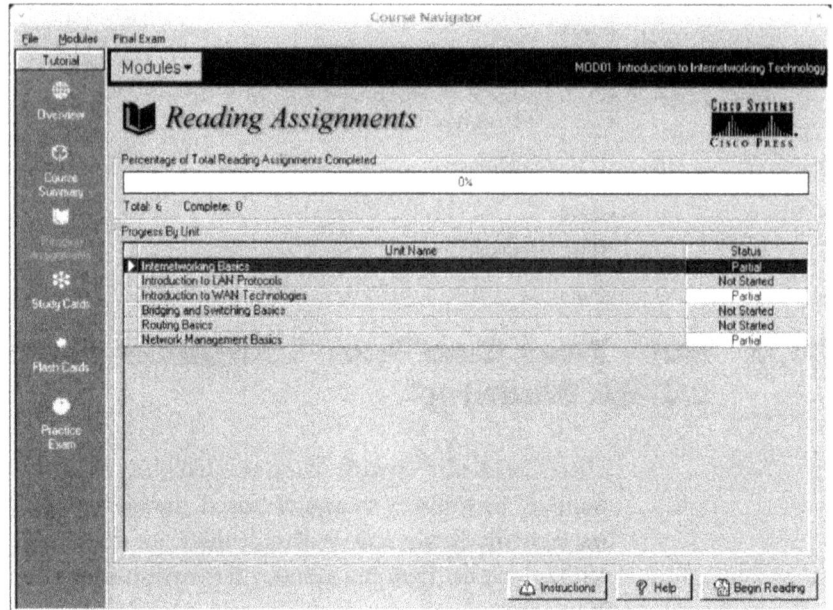

Figure 10.5
*CCNA Complete
Reading
Assignment.*

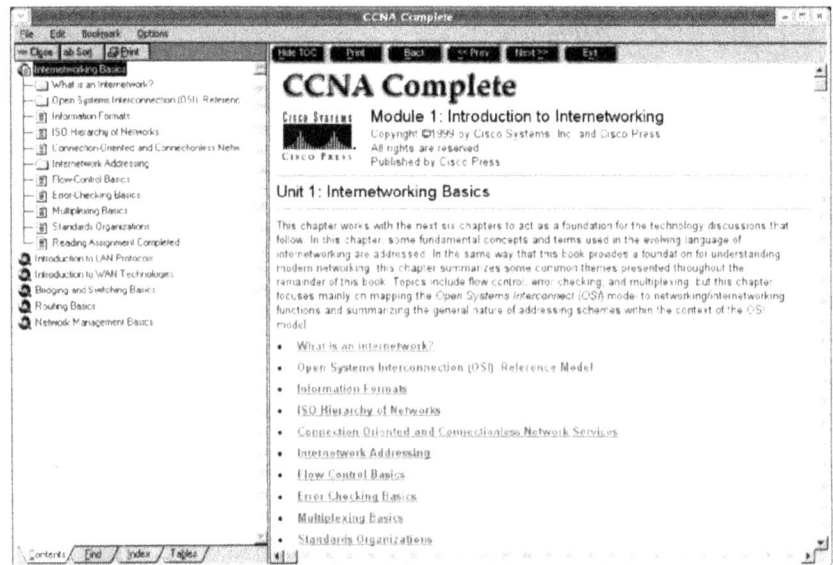

In addition to the reading material, the tests and study cards (Figure 10.6) also work as expected.

With one slight change it is now possible to use CCNA Complete on your Linux desktop via an interpreter.

Figure 10.6
CCNA Complete
Study Cards.

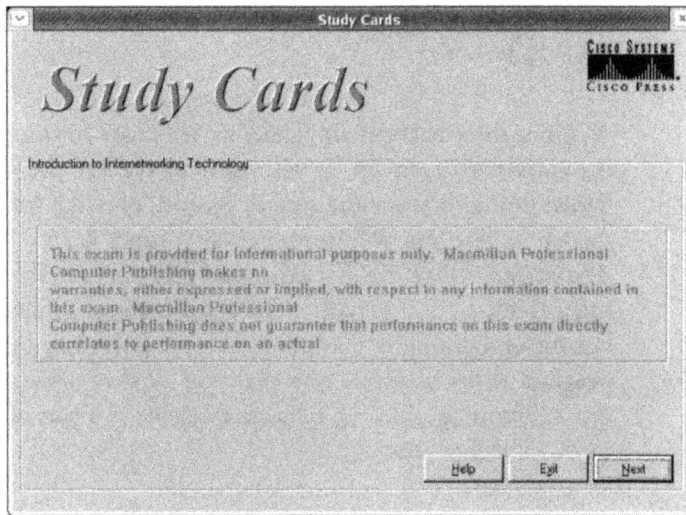

10.4.2   Sybex CCNAGold Virtual Router Lab Software

Due to limitations in Wine's handling of encrypted filesystems, the only method available to use this training tool is via VMware; even though the installation works, the data is inaccessible.

10.4.3   Cisco CCNA Network Simulator

The Cisco CCNA Network Simulator is an invaluable tool for learning about the Cisco product line, with the ability to simulate complex networks. Because of this, we should see if it runs on Linux. Actually, since it's a Windows program, we want to determine if we require VMWare to run this program or can we use Wine, which is not as expensive.

First, install the Cisco CCNA Network Simulator using Wine's installation tool. Once you do that, you will also need to do the following:

```
cp -rp /mnt/cdrom/program\ files/Cisco\ CCNA\ Network\
Simulator/ ~/.cxoffice/Program\ Files
```

Edit the file ~/.cxoffice/config and add the following lines to the end before the # [/wineconf] marker.

```
[AppDefaults\\Boson_NetSim.exe\\x11drv]
"Desktop" = "800x600"
"Managed" = "Y"
```

```
[AppDefaults\\nlab menu.exe\\x11drv]
"Desktop" = "800x600"
"Managed" = "Y"
```

Once these changes are made, we are ready to run the simulator. When the simulator starts up, it will want to register the tool with ciscopress. When doing this, use the second option, over the Internet, but not automated, or else you will never get the proper license key to type into the next screen. Once this happens, you can then see the virtual lab environment (Figure 10.7) as well as the actual courses to take (Figure 10.8). The last bit of warning is that the CBT will warn you that the default telnet program is not available and that you need to set a new one. Do not set this to anything, since no telnet is available as a part of Wine; the CBT has its own mechanisms.

Figure 10.7
CCNA Network Simulator Login.

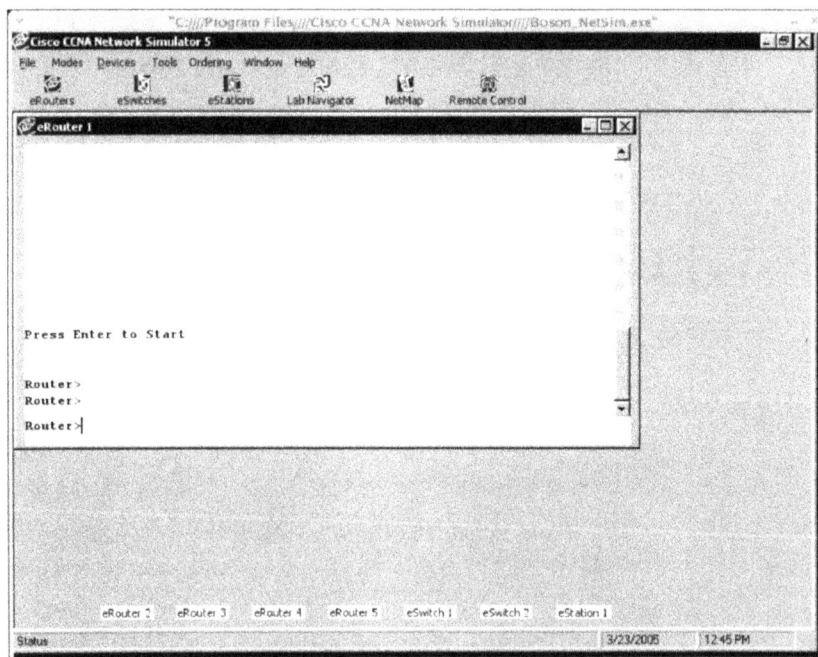

Another gotcha is that the mouse will not always select the lab to run, but once you click into the column with the list of labs the mouse keys will traverse to each lab, the enter key will start the lab, and the mouse will work perfectly once into the lab or reading.

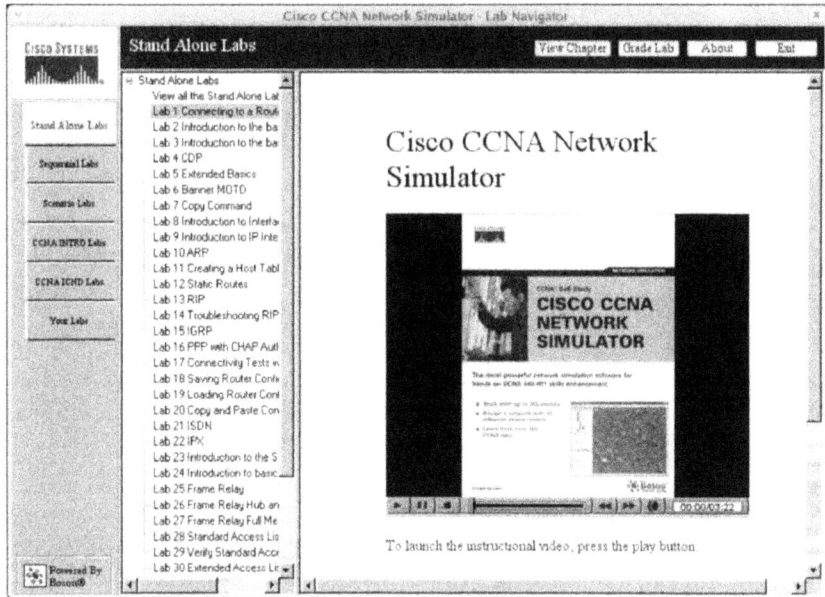

Figure 10.8
CCNA Network Simulator Course Navigator.

10.5 The Cost

As can be seen, there are not many Linux-only options for training. There are a few and it's a growing list, but there is nothing in the mainstream yet. However, that is not the end of everything, because using inexpensive tools such as CrossOver Office can bring CBT and other training tools to the desktop.

10.6 Support

Training tools, under CrossOver Office, are not necessarily supported by CodeWeavers or even the tool vendor, so using these training tools could be a risk. However, the Wine open source community is very active and can answer your questions. With a little investigation into wine and how to solve its problems, many of the issues faced can easily be solved with those tools not dependent upon .NET. Any .NET tool in Wine will fail, since it is not yet supported.

10.7 Conclusion

Since most training is currently delivered over the Web, many of the training-enabling tools are already a part of Linux (review chapter 4); with the use of Wine, even more tools become available for use. The use of CBT training for Windows on Linux will require Wine or VMWare and gives a reusable source of training materials without a great expenditure of monies or even time. However, I freely admit that learning the ins and outs of Wine is not for the faint of heart and can easily be misleading. Intuition will guide you, as well as an understanding of how the programs work. (see Table 10.1)

Table 10.1   *Current Software Information*

Software	Support Level	Fee	Support Fee
VMware	Web Based/Phone	$199	Free for 90 days
Mozilla	OpenSource	NA	NA
CrossOver Office	Web Based	$60	Free for 90 days
WebEX Player	Web Based	NA	NA
CCNA Complete	Web Based	$150	NA
Cisco CCNA Network Simulator	Web Based	$300+	NA

An Investigative Approach

It took many years of research to discover all the applications outlined in the previous chapters. Mainly, once deciding what to research, it took time to find all the possible options to solve the problem of how to implement the application in question. It many not sound difficult, but there are currently at least 14,000 possible open-source projects and countless for fee products out there for Linux, while only at most 6,000 packages are shipped with any Linux distribution. In some cases Linux tools grew to overwhelm for-fee products. For example, Red Hat 3.0.3 shipped with a for fee version of X while now Red Hat ships with an open-source version of the software.

With all these open-source projects, there is quite a bit of research to perform for each application, so the big question is where to start. To overcome this hindrance and the numerous packages, a process was devised to organize each possible solution to the integration problem.

11.1 The Process

11.1.1 Gather Requirements

As outlined in Chapter 1, review your requirements for the application in question. If you know which part of the application is unused, is a nice thing to have, a not heavily used portion, and is a must have, then you can adequately create criteria for gathering information about and judging possible solutions.

11.1.2 Start the Search

Starting your search can be a harrowing experience at times, so start the search review of your Linux distribution for packages that may already fit your bill.

11.1.3   Expand the Search

Visit Web sites for other Linux distributions, since there is a chance that there is a pre-built or source package that will work with your distribution. For example Fedora Core 3 packages can be used with RHEL4 installations if necessary. Also, visit sites such as http://www.freshmeat.net, http://www.sourceforge.net, http://www.rpmfind.net, and http://www.google.com/linux. Last, review the Linux magazines *Linux World, Linux Journal, Linux Format*, and *Info World* (there are quite a few other magazines that are useful but these are the major ones). Once you have gathered up possible solutions to the application in question, you will want to add to your list the use of Wine as an interpreted solution.

11.1.4   Test Your Solutions

Now that you have your requirements and possible solutions, you should install and test your solutions to see which best fits your needs; include in this test the supportability of the solution, the difficulty it takes to install, and possible existing precompiled packages that contain the solution. Third, party locations for packages include http://www.rpmfind.net, http://dag.wieers.com/home-made/apt, http://freshrpms.net, http://newrpms.sunsite.dk, http://rpm.pbone.net, and http://www.rpmseek.com.

11.2   Implement Your Solutions

Now that a list of possible solutions has been defined and your tests completed, we need to implement the solutions. Install into /usr/local if necessary or build RPMs for your distribution for easier upgrades.

11.3   Sanity Check

With so many options available, you should sanity check your solution for being a modern tool with possible maintenance and support; it would not be good if you chose a tool that has not been updated in five years! Also be sure to consider Wine as an option. At this time, you may want to visit other options as well that may have become available since the start of your research.

11.4 Work with Open-Source Communities

If you see something in an open-source project that should be fixed or is a bug, please run through the mailing lists for the project and see if it's been spotted before and if there is a solution; otherwise, file a bug report so that it will get fixed by the community. An example is the gphoto package. I require a version that works for a Canon EOS 20D and the current ones do not work. This has been covered in the mailing lists for that project and it is fixed in the source pool, but a release is not available yet.

11.5 Stay in Sync or Keep up-to-date

In some cases, a solution may not have everything you need, so you will need to constantly watch these packages for updates or for new packages that can fill the same role. As an example:

- With the advent of the RHEL4 release of Red Hat Enterprise Linux Distribution there are newer packages that are now part of the distribution while others are still lacking. My list of necessary additions include:

  - RealPlayer—Ships on the Extras CD now and as part of the standard distribution of HelixPlayer, an OpenSource media player that is sponsored by Real but does not play everything yet.
  - Acrobat Reader—Ships on the Extras CD now but is still at an older revision.
  - Java—Ships in two forms on the Extras CD now. Either the IBM Java or the BEA Java is now available.
  - mplayer—mplayer is available from http://dag.wieers.com/home-made/apt as a precompiled RPM for RHEL4.
  - xine— This is needed to play Windows Media WMX files. I get this from http://dag.wieers.com/home-made/apt as well.
  - gnucash—I use gnucash for my home accounting, but there is no method to build this yet on RHEL4. The RHEL3 approach is the best approach, except that the gal package required by gnucash has build issues. Instead of rebuilding the packages necessary to get gnucash working, the Fedora Core 3 packages were used. The source for gnucash can be found at http://www.gnucash.org.

    ```
    bonobo-1.0.22-9.i386.rpm

    gal-0.24-4.i386.rpm
    ```

```
GConf-1.0.9-15.i386.rpm

gdk-pixbuf-gnome-0.22.0-15.0.i386.rpm

gnome-print-0.37-10.i386.rpm

gnome-vfs-1.0.5-21.i386.rpm

gnucash-1.8.9-2.i386.rpm

gnucash-backend-postgres-1.8.9-2.i386.rpm

gtkhtml-1.1.9-10.i386.rpm

Guppi-0.40.3-21.i386.rpm

g-wrap-1.3.4-7.i386.rpm

libgal23-0.24-4.i386.rpm

libghttp-1.0.9-10.i386.rpm

libglade-0.17-15.i386.rpm

libgnomeprint15-0.37-10.i386.rpm

libofx-0.6.6-2.i386.rpm

libxml-1.8.17-11.i386.rpm

oaf-0.6.10-11.i386.rpm

openhbci-0.9.17-1.i386.rpm

rpm -ivh *rpm
```

- gphoto2—I need v2.1.16 (which does not exist yet) to get support for my Canon EOS 20D, so I use the latest source from the CVS (Concurrent Version System) repository at http://www.gphoto.org as a starting place until a real release is ready. Granted, starting from source can be difficult, but it is necessary from time to time. The gimp-gtkam plug-in does not build or install properly yet. To build gphoto the following must be used after downloading the source per the Web site.

```
Download From CVS

cd libgphoto2

sh autogen.sh

./configure

ln -s /usr/share/automake-1.9/mkinstalldirs .

cd libgphoto_port
```

```
ln -s /usr/share/automake-1.9/mkinstalldirs .

cd ..

make rpm

cd packaging/rpm/RPMS/i386

rpm -e gphoto2 gphoto2-devel

rpm -ivh *.rpm


cd gphoto2

sh autogen.sh

./configure

ln -s /usr/share/automake-1.9/mkinstalldirs .

make dist

cd packaging/rpm

Edit Makefile and change rpm to be rpmbuild

make rpm

cd RPMS/i386

rpm -ivh *rpm


cd gtkam

sh autogen.sh

./configure

ln -s /usr/share/automake-1.9/mkinstalldirs .

make install

cd /etc/hotplug/usb/


cp libusbscanner usbcam
```

- gimp-perl—In order to display gimp files gimp-perl is required for the xcdtopnm package. Unfortunately, gimp-perl does not yet exist for RHEL4. I will either have to install direct from CPAN (http://www.cpan.org) or try the Fedora Core 3 versions.

- mozplugger—Mozplugger (http://mozplugger.mozdev.org) is a replacement for the necessary package Plugger v5.1.3 that has better support for Firefox, since it is better maintained. Chapter 4 goes into detail about plugger, and since mozplugger is based on plugger the chapter still applies. However, the configuration file code is very different and not everything in Plugger exists in mozplugger so be sure to test your needs.

- Instant Messenger—There are other unified instant messengers not mentioned in Chapter 5. These include Kopete (http://kopete.kde.org) (KDE version similar to GAIM [http://gaim.sourceforge.net], NAIM (http://naim.n.ml.org) (command line interface version of GAIM), and CenterICQ (http://centericq.de) (more than just ICQ), as well as the mentioned tools. Since GAIM ships as a part of RHEL4, no other tool is necessary; however, AYTTM also works fine after a recompile. There are many more, and *Linux Format March 2005* has a very good article on the pros and cons of each.

- Wine—CodeWeavers' version of Wine provides a corporate supported version of the interpreter. Installation of my typical Windows tools (Office, Visio, etc.) on my RHEL4 laptop makes it easy to integrate into the office. With v4.2 coming out from http://www.codeweavers.com there is a good chance that my CCNA training applications may work better.

- Cabextract and necessary fonts—The cabextract (mentioned in Chapter 3) package and its fonts have not changed and they install just fine on RHEL4.

- AntiVirus software—Clamav installed from http://dag.wieers.com/home-made/apt works just fine for RHEL4.

- Access tools—mdbtools still has a limitation in that it will not write to Access databases, but it has even more of a limitation on RHEL4; it will not compile due to issues with Gnome release differences, and we may have to investigate Fedora Core 3 possibilities.

- Web editing—Quanta is now the KDEWebDev package and still does not work well with FrontPage.

- Palm integration—My Tungsten T3 works quite well with the stock programs from RHEL4; however, the Clie PEG-N710 has issues with Gpilotd but not pilot-link or Jpilot.

- Terminal programs—xterm still works fine and the latest version of rdesktop is now a part of RHEL4, making this easier to install and use. While PowerTerm installs, I prefer to use xterm for these types of things. In addition, RHEL4 now ships with x3270 as an IBM Host Access tool.

- Wireless—The Orinoco_usb module is not yet part of the 2.6 kernel, so use of DKMS and module source is still required.

As you can see, staying on top of your requirements as new releases are made gains you a plan on moving forward. In some cases, I will need to investigate alternative source pools to gain the functionality I require, while others are now a part of the Linux distribution. With every new release of critical software and Linux distribution, it is recommended that each of your applications be reviewed for upgrades and newer features and even newer packages.

11.6 Process Implementation

Let us now take an example application and see how it fits into the outlined process.

11.6.1 How Can I create Architectural Views on Linux?

The best-known architectural drawing programs may not be available for Linux (i.e., AutoCad) but there are many others. When we follow our process, we are first going to look at requirements and then move on to solutions.

Requirements

- Integrate with AutoCad—that is, read and export DXF files
- Be easy to use
- Preferably open-source
- Provide a good library of standard shapes and items
- Plane view is required (2D flat view as if looking at a blueprint)
- 3D view would be nice

Start the search

RHEL4 provides the following graphics programs:

- Gimp (more a Photoshop equivalent)
- Run the following commands on distribution:

- apropos draw
- apropos graphics
- apropos drafting
- apropos architect
- apropos figures
- apropos cad

- Xfig is a simple figure drawing program

11.6.2   Expand the Search

Since RHEL4's distribution did not leave us much information, we need to progress outward. We should check the Fedora Core 3 Web site for possible matches, since it's the closest thing to RHEL4. However, that will not lead to many possibilities we have already found. Time to hit the Web sites. First, we try the repositories:

- The ATrpms repository contains Skencil, which is similar to xfig. Still not very useful, so we expand further and search http://www.google.com/linux for "CAD Programs" and get an immediate hit for Linux Gazette (http://www.linuxgazette.com/issue54/frost.html), which is a reputable site for Linux information. Since it's dated in 2000, it is a bit old. However, the packages mentioned are interesting.

  - Qcad
  - CAM Expert
  - SISCAD-P
  - ME10
  - CADDA
  - Varicad
  - Microstation
  - Varimetrix

- A better link may be http://www.linuxlinks.com/Software/Graphics/CAD/index.shtml, which lists many more possible solutions to the problem, including many commercial programs such as Pro/Engineer.

- Now that we have a good list of possible solutions to the question, we need to review each one to fit the requirements; since we desire open-source solutions it removes any commercial product from the list. Then we need to go through what is left and find one that is recently updated and has an active community. One such is Qcad. While freeCAD looks promising, there is no mention of DXF import/export in the brief documentation.

11.6.3 Implement Your Solution

Qcad (http://www.ribbonsoft.com/qcad.html) comes in two flavors. One is the free community-supported source code and the other is a small fee-supported version of the software. Checking out the limitations on operating systems shows that it may not run on RHEL4.

Verify that QT is installed on the system using:

```
rpm –q qt-devel
```

Then verify that qmake is available:

```
qmake –v
```

Then unpack the source and build:

```
tar –xzf qcad-2.0.4.0-1.src.tar.gz

cd qcad-2.0.4.0-1.src

cd scripts

./build_qcad.sh
```

Now execute:

```
cd ../qcad

./qcad
```

Installation into /opt/qcad or /usr/local is achieved by copying the qcad directory to the directory by hand and then pointing the configuration to the new directory.

Once we have the program running, save and open dialogs show that it will read and write various forms of DXF files, which meets our requirements. In addition, my test DXF file reads in just fine. So this becomes a successful tool for 2D drafting with no bells and whistles. There is, in addition, a large parts library accessible off the download page for Qcad, which meets another one of our requirements. Since Qcad deals primarily with basic shapes, it is relatively easy to use.

Supportability is the next concern. Since the code is open-source you can purchase a prebuilt release for a minor support fee of roughly $28 to receive one year of support.

11.6.4 Sanity Check

As a sanity check, we should review whether there are any other options available. There are many options available but none has the same abilities as Qcad, which is a modern project with a viable community and a company that will offer support for a small fee. In addition, while you can try to get AutoCad to work under Wine, there is no good success story at this time. Another option is Visio via Wine, but that is also not a drafting tool and will not read or write DXF files.

11.6.5 Work with the Open-Source Community

Since Qcad is an ongoing open-source project, you can send e-mail to the mailing lists and monitor them for fixes to various bugs. While not a very chatty e-mail list, it does have some extremely good information. The mailing list location is documented on the home page for Qcad (as it is with many projects).

11.6.6 Stay in Sync or Keep up-to-date

Bookmark the Web site for Qcad and check it for updates. Since this is not part of a repository of projects, you will need to do this by hand and check every so often—perhaps only when you need a fix or even when new patches come out for your Linux Distribution. I have been using Qcad for several releases so have been monitoring this site for updates.

We have now successfully solved the problem. The solution is to use Qcad and the question was: How can I create architectural views on Linux? Every must-have requirement was met while the nice-to-have requirement was not. Qcad is not a 3D modeling engine, that would be a different search criterion. While AutoCad Architectural would be extremely nice to have to get the full 3D view, a simple plane view gives a builder or contractor the necessary information to create exactly what is required.

11.7 Conclusion

While following this process will find answers to your questions it is by no means the only method you can use; however, it is the one followed for the proceding chapters of this book. Since there is such a wide range of possible packages to review, the use of these guidelines will quickly target possible solutions to your questions about specific applications. Remember to include supportability as a part of your research. Not only do things have to work, they should be supportable in some fashion.

11.8   The Cost

The cost of using Qcad over other tools is just the fee for the commercial version of the software; otherwise, since it's OpenSource it is easy to get, compile, and run.

11.9   Support

For $28 per annum you can get e-mail support for this application in its commercial form. This form is not as up-to-date as the source, but it is in a form that is supportable by Ribbon Soft.

11.10 Conclusion

While Qcad does not yet provide a 3D drafting environment, its existing features and parts library are extremely well done and quite large. Being able to interact with AutoCad is a huge bonus as well (see Table 11.1).

Table 11.1   *Qcad Information*

Software	Support Level	Fee	Support Fee
Qcad	Web Based/E-mail	$28	NA

12

Conclusion and Future Directions

While this book tries to answer the most common issues regarding the use of Linux as a valid corporate desktop, it is by no means complete. New challenges and questions arise every day regarding all desktops, and I will continue to pursue these in the realm of Linux. If you would like to pose a question, provide feedback, and even new solutions to be presented in a future edition of this book or on the Web site related to this book, please send e-mail to books@astroarch.com or visit the Web site http://www.astroarch.com/~elh/books.html. I freely admit that there are other books covering much of the material in more detail than is presented here; however, we are trying to present only the detail required to install the product to meet the specified needs for an integrated desktop, as well as the costs of use.

In addition, many items show limitations in Linux; these are not necessarily limitations, but questions that the administrators and managers must ask about how their network and desktops will be used. Each chapter covers a wide range of tools and possible implementation options, and it is up to the system designers to ask the right questions and plan for success. Planning ahead and asking the tough questions up front will save in support and implementation costs later. To prove the usability of the tools mentioned herein, this book was written using them: Word via CrossOver Office, StarOffice, OpenOffice, and Documents-To-Go on a Palm handheld device, as well as other Linux tools.

Support costs are associated with every implementation of a desktop. The worst-case scenario could be the loss of warranty support from the distribution vendor, as happens when the kernel is recompiled to add a necessary feature such as IPSec NAT-T support. While this is not desirable, it nonetheless could be the result if the kernel is tainted, and plans must be made in advance to debug any issue using only vendor-supplied software and patches. The support costs could be the limiting factor; however, those who use Linux on the desktop can generally fix their own problems within the confines of IT guidelines.

To conclude this book is difficult, as it grows daily; however, there are a few handy conclusions we can draw. First, using Linux on the desktop is no more complex in many ways than using Windows on the desktop. Similar tools are available for each system, although there is a learning curve for support personnel who do not currently support Linux. While this book shows ways to implement, work with, and interoperate with other operating systems, you will want to standardize your tools, and you should plan in advance which tools will be part of your Linux desktop.

Step back to Chapter 1 for a moment, where we asked the questions:

1.   Is Linux ready for real use as a desktop?

2.   Is Linux ready to be used as a corporate desktop?

The easy answer to both is yes, Linux is ready; but, as demonstrated in this book, the practical implementation is much more complex and must be based on your specific desktop requirements. Looking at our example:

Your corporate environment uses Microsoft Office, yet you do not need Access, Visio, or FrontPage. However, use of e-mail, Word, and Excel is paramount. In addition, you have network printers as well as Windows-based file servers. Everyone in the office has a PalmOS device of some type. Web content is generally simple, with shared Word or Excel documents available. Last, IRC is the interoffice communication tool of choice.

We end up with the table of requirements shown in Table 10.1.

As discussed, there are many tools to accomplish the tasks required, and knowing which tools are available and any limitations or advantages is a boon to those designing a desktop and identifying all the costs involved. When using Linux as your desktop, you can make many choices. You will want to choose a distribution of Linux that offers the best level of support for your needs. Some come preconfigured for the best Linux-based integration (as is the case with the Xandros distribution of Linux).

Table 12.1   *Requirements for a Linux-based System*

Software	Linux Equivalents	Caveats
Word/Excel	OpenOffice	Issue with compatibility to Word/Excel No esoteric plug-in support
	StarOffice	Similar to OpenOffice, but with paid support
	CrossOver Office	Runs Word/Excel via Wine—no esoteric plugin support
	VMware	Full Word/Excel
Exchange	Evolution	Cannot access shared mailboxes
	Mozilla (OWA)	Takes up screen real estate
	Crossover Office	Runs Outlook via Wine. No esoteric plug-in support
	VMware	Full Outlook
Printing	CUPS via SMB/network interface	Full access to printer
File Sharing	Via Nautilus	Access to all shares, yet password required every time, and no program access
	Via smbmount	Passwords in cleartext file
	VMware	Standard Windows
	Via NFS	No special Windows clients required
Palm Desktop/ HotSync	gnome-pilot/Evolution	Full main memory HotSync—no external card support
	Documents-To-Go	Special script to synchronize Documents To Go and photos to Palm main memory
	VMware	Full access to HotSync/Palm desktop
Web Browser	Mozilla	Many standard plug-ins
	OpenOffice	Adds more Windows-specific plug-ins for use
	VMware	Standard Windows

Table 12.1   *Requirements for a Linux-based System (continued)*

Software	Linux Equivalents	Caveats
IRC	Xchat	Linux native client
	Mozilla	Limited, but with aggressive notifications
	CrossOver Office	mIRC client
Antivirus/Spam Filter	MailScanner with Spam-Assassin and ClamAV	Open-source tools to protect sendmail with a Bayesian learning engine for spam blocking.
Support	While some of these tools are open source, all the projects are extremely active and responsive. Their respective vendors support the other tools. In the case of spam filters and antivirus protection, there are a number of vendors from which to choose. In addition, these vendors can support your distribution.	

To conclude, plan ahead, ask the tough questions up front, and your Linux desktop will be stable, supportable, and usable.

13

My Recipe

The preceding chapters and following appendices outline many new features and aspects of Linux that enable us to answer the question: Will Linux work as a corporate desktop? Furthermore, we have progressed through a series of discussions based around the concept of integration with *no* migration to Linux. In other words, the philosophy of this book is:

Linux can be integrated into an existing networked environment of mixed computing machines and operating systems in such a way that there is a seamless use of necessary applications.

For RedHat Enterprise Linux 4, I used the following recipe on my own machine.

13.1 Ingredients

Network Access

RHEL4WS Media CD-ROMs/DVD-ROM

RHEL4WS Extras CD-ROM

Knowledge of Linux build and configure tools

13.2 Steps

1. Install RHEL4WS, ensuring that the development environment is also installed. Install using Software Raid across two like hard disks.

2.   On reboot after installation, install the contents of the RHEL4WS Extras CD-ROM.

3.   Upgrade RHEL4WS to the latest versions of all software using the Red Hat Network and the up2date tool.

4.   Install and configure YUM (http://dag.wieers.com/packages/yum/). Specifically download the source RPM, and use rpmrebuild to rebuild the RPM for installation on RHEL4.

5.   Configure the /etc/yum.conf to point to the RHEL4 entries for the Dag Wieers RPM repository by adding the following lines:

```
[dag]
name=Dag RPM Repository for RHEL
baseurl=http://apt.sw.be/redhat/el4/en/i386/dag
```

6.   Using YUM, specifically install some extra software from the Dag Wieers repository using the following command. You should note that some security software mentioned in this list is not discussed in the book; this is the way I harden my machines.

```
yum install mplayer mplayer-skins mplayer-fonts xine
clamav clamav-db clamd clamtk chkrootkit kino perl-
Curses perl-Tk yumi
```

7.   Compile and install libsidplay, as well as sidplay-base, as described in Chapter 4. In addition, make an RPM using the CheckInstall (http://asic-linux.com.mx/~izto/checkinstall/) tool. CheckInstall, while not mentioned in this book, is a new tool that replaces "make install" and will build installable packages for Debian-, Slackware-, and RPM-based distributions.

8.   Using rpmrebuild, rebuild and install the Xanim RPM, as described in Chapter 4.

9.   Compile and install FreeWRL, as described in Chapter 4, using the CheckInstall tool.

10.   Configure and test all the Firefox plug-ins using the plugger testing grounds at http://fredrik.hubbe.net/plugger/test.html. Be sure to make the additions required for the WMX multimedia format discussed in Chapter 10. Fix or make note of any problems that may appear. The testing grounds mention the Linspire

testing grounds as well. Linspire is a very good location to test further your Firefox configuration.

11. Install DKMS v2 RPM from http://linux.dell.com/dkms/.

12. Install the Orinoco USB v0.2.2 drivers into DKMS, as described in Chapter 2.

13. Install the Microsoft core fonts, as described in Chapter 3. Cabextract is also available via the Dag Wieers RPM Repository.

14. Install GNUcash, as described in Chapter 8 and in the RHEL4 update in Chapter 10.

15. Install gphoto update, as described in Chapter 8 and in the RHEL4 update in Chapter 10.

16. Install WordPerfect, as described in Chapter 3.

17. Install Qcad, as described in Chapter 11.

18. Install new-kdewebdev (quanta replacement), as described in the RHEL4 update in Chapter 10.

19. Install xkeycaps and vmsterm as described in Chapter 7.

20. Install CrossOver Office, as described in Appendix A. Inside CrossOver Office, install:

    a. Internet Explorer 6

    b. All the "free" viewers from the CrossOver Office setup screens

    c. Microsoft Office 2000

    d. Microsoft FrontPage 2000

    e. Microsoft Visio 2000

    f. QuickBooks Pro 1999

    g. CCNA training materials

21. Harden the system using Bastille (http://www.bastillelinux.org).

22. Install corporate-specific Windows and Linux tools:

    a. VPN

    b. Call management

    c. Internal communications tools

23.   Configure the Evolution e-mail client for e-mail and Palm integration.

24.   Install the par tool and Documents To Go script, as described in Chapter 8.

25.   Make a recovery CD using either mondo (http://www.microwerks.net/~hugo/) or mkcdrec. While mondo was not mentioned extensively in this book, it is another recovery mechanism with a more user-friendly interface than mkcdrec. Also, mkbootdisk can be used to create a necessary boot disk to recover the system from the software raid in use.

Stir all the ingredients or follow these steps, bake for roughly three hours at 350 degrees, and you will have a system that will provide an integrated Linux environment!

Glossary

123	Lotus 1-2-3 document
AbiWord	Microsoft rich text format (RTF) writer
acroread	Adobe Acrobat Reader (ftp://download.adobe.com/pub/adobe/acrobatreader/unix/)
AIM	AOL Instant Messaging protocol and network
AlsaPlayer	Multimedia player using the ALSA sound system for Linux
ANIM?	Xanim (X Animator) media format
artsplay	ARTS daemon sound player (man artsplay)
ASF	Windows Media format
ASX	Windows Media format
AU	Basic audio multimedia format
AVI	Microsoft video media format
awk	Linux command for manipulating files
cabextract	Open-source Linux tool for extracting Microsoft CAB files (http://core-fonts.sourceforge.net)
CCNA	Cisco Certified Network Associate
ChatZilla	Mozilla IRC client
chkfontpath	Linux command for verifying X font paths (man chkfontpath)
chmod	Linux command for modifying permissions on files or directories (man chmod)

CIFS	Common Internet File System (http://www.ubiqx.org/cifs)
ClamAV	Open-source antivirus software (http://clamav.elektrapro.com)
codecs	Bits of code that will interpret multimedia content for movie players compiled into bytecode
cp	Linux copy command (man cp)
CrossOver	Commercial version of Wine (http://www.codeweavers.com)
DKMS	Dynamic Kernel Module System
dlpsh	Pilotlink Shell for manipulating a PDA
DL	Video Media format
DNS	Domain name service (man bind)
DOC	Microsoft Word document
dos2unix	Command to convert MS-DOS text files to UNIX text files (man dos2unix)
DOT	Microsoft Word template document
drakconf	Configuration tool for Mandrake Linux
DriverLoader	For-fee Linux tool for using Windows Ndis wireless network drivers with Linux (http://www.linuxant.com)
DVD	Digital Video Disc
DVI	Device-independent file
elm	Old Linux mail client
esdplay	ESD daemon sound player (man esdplay)
Evolution	Graphical mail client
ext2	Linux extended filesystem 2
ext3	Linux extended filesystem 3
fi	Linux Bourne Shell or Bourne Again Shell command language for ending an if clause (man bash)
flashplayer	Macromedia Flash Player (http://macromedia.com/shockwave/download/alternates)

FLC	Animation format developed by Autodesk, Inc.
FLI	Animation format developed by Autodesk, Inc.
FreeWRL	Free Web Reality engine software (http://freewrl.sourceforge.net/)
FrontPage	Microsoft Web page development program
FTP	File Transfer Protocol
GAIM	Instant messaging client for multiple protocols (http://gaim.sourceforge.net)
gcc	GNU C Compiler (man gcc)
Gentoo	Linux distribution
Ghostscript	PostScript viewer program (man ghostscript)
gmplayer	Graphical movie player (mplayer GUI)
Gnome	Graphical user interface for X
GnomeMeeting	Gnome video conferencing client (http://www.gnomemeeting.org)
GnuCash	Tool for tracking personal finances (http://www.gnucash.com)
Gnumeric	GNU spreadsheet
gphoto	Tool for downloading pictures from a digital camera (http://www.gphoto.org)
gv	GhostView viewer for PDF files
HelixPlayer	Open-source version of RealPlayer
HFS	Hierarchical file system used by older Apple computers
HotSync	The act of backing up or placing files onto a PDA
IBMJava	Java from IBM for Linux
ICQ	Instant messaging protocol and network
IMAP	Internet message access protocol
IPSec	Internet protocol security
IRC	Internet relay chat
ISO 9660	Common format for CD-ROMs

Jabber	Instant messaging protocol and network
Java	Bytecode-based interpreted language that requires all code to be
KDE	X Windows user interface
Konqueror	KDE Web browser
LAN	Local Area Network
ln	Linux command for making symbolic and hard links between files (man ln)
M3U	MPEG music resource locator
MailScanner	Tool for stopping e-mail SPAM and viruses (http://www.sng.ecs.soton.ac.uk/mailscanner/)
make	Linux build tool (man make)
man	Linux command for accessing the online manual (man man)
mcd	mtools command for changing to a specified directory on an MS-DOS-formatted floppy disk (man mcd)
mcopy	mtools command to copy files in MS-DOS format (man mcopy)
MDB	Microsoft Database Format
mdir	mtools command for listing MSDOS formatted directories (man mdir)
mformat	mtools command for formatting a floppy as an MS-DOS diskette (man mformat)
MIDI	Digital audio multimedia format
MikMod	SoundTracker audio multimedia player
mIRC	Microsoft Windowsñbased IRC Client
mkdir	Linux shell command for making directories (man bash)
mkfontdir	Linux tool to make font directories usable by X (man mkfontdir)
MOVIE	SGI video media format
MOV	QuickTime movie media format
Mozilla	Linux Web browser (http://www.mozilla.org)
MozillaMail	Linux Web browser mail client

mozplugger	New tool based on plugger (http://mozplugger.mozdev.org)
MP3	MPEG audio version 3
MPA	MPEG audio multimedia format
MPEG2	Multimedia video format version 2
MPEG	Multimedia video format
MPlayer	Movie player (http://www.mplayerhq.hu/homepage)
MSN	Microsoft instant messaging protocol and network
mtools	MS-DOS package for accessing MS-DOS–based floppies
multisession	Format for a CD-ROM that hosts multiple copies of files
MUTT	Mail client for Linux
NAT	Network Address Translation
NAT-T	Network Address Translation Traversal
Nautilus	Gnome graphical file viewer
NDIS	Windows driver for network cards
NdisWrapper	Tool to use Windows NDIS wireless network drivers on Linux (http://ndiswrapper.sourceforge.net)
netatalk	Net AppleTalk (Open-source AppleTalk suite)
NetMeeting	Microsoft video conferencing client
NFS	Network File System
NTFS	Windows NT File System
OGG	Vorbis streaming video/audio media format
oocalc	OpenOffice Spreadsheet/Excel writer
ooimpress	OpenOffice Impress/PowerPoint writer
oomath	OpenOffice Math writer
oowriter	OpenOffice Document writer

OpenH323	Open Source H323 Protocol video conferencing tools (http://www.openh323.org)
P2P	Peer-to-peer communication
par	Palm ARchiver tool for translating files into streamed palm data files (http://www.djw.org/product/palm/par)
PBM	Portable Bitmap Media file format
PDA	Personal Digital Assistant
PDB	Protein Data Bank file
PDF	Portable Document Format
Perl	Practical Extraction and Report Language
PGM	Portable Greymap Media file format
PINE	Mail client
PLS	SHOUTcast playlist
plugger	Plug-in manager for Mozilla (http://fredrik.hubbe.net/plugger.html)
plug-in	Bits of code separate from any application, yet unable to run unless the other application is in use. Plug-ins add functionality to other applications
PNM	Portable Anymap Media file format
PowerTerm	X-based terminal emulator that features support for many terminal protocols (http://www.ericom.com/pti.asp)
PPM	Portable Pixmap Media file format
PPT	Microsoft PowerPoint slideshow
PPTP	Point-to-Point Protocol
PSD	Photoshop image format
PS	PostScript format
QCad	Simple 2D CAD program (http://www.ribbonsoft.com/qcad.html)
QT	QuickTime movie media format
Quanta	KDE Web page development program

RAM	Real Audio Multimedia format
RA	Real Audio Multimedia format
rdesktop	Remote desktop tool for Linux (http://www.rdesktop.org)
RealPlayer	Player for Real Media file formats (http://scopes.real.com/real/player/unix/unix.html)
redhat-config-network	Red Hat network configuration tool
redhat-config-printer	Red Hat printer configuration tool
Red Hat	Linux distribution
RM	Real Media multimedia format
rpmbuild	Linux command to rebuild RPM packages from the source package
RPM	RealPlayer Plug-in Metafile multimedia format
RPM	Red Hat Package Manager
RTF	Rich Text Format
RV	Real Video multimedia format
SDA	StarDraw document
SDC	StarCalc document
SDD	OpenOffice Impress document
SDP	OpenOffice Impress Packed document
SDW	StarWriter document
SGL	StarWriter Global document
SID	Commodore 64 audio multimedia format
SIDPLAY	Commodore 64 multimedia player (http://www.geocities.com/SiliconValley/Lakes/5147/sidplay)
smbmount	Mount a CIFS
SMB	Server Message Block protocol
SMF	StarMath document

SMI	RealPlayer multimedia format
SpamAssassin	Tool for stopping spam e-mail
SpamBouncer	Tool for stopping spam e-mail (http://www.spambouncer.org)
SSH	Secure SHell (man ssh)
STC	OpenOffice Calc Template document
STD	OpenOffice Draw Template document
STI	OpenOffice Impress Template document
STW	OpenOffice Writer Template document
SuSE	Linux distribution
SXC	OpenOffice Calc document
SXD	OpenOffice Draw document
SXG	OpenOffice Writer Global document
SXM	OpenOffice Math document
SXW	OpenOffice Writer document
system-config-net-work	Red Hat network configuration tool
tar	Tape ARchive Linux command (man tar)
TIFF	Tagged Image File Format
TiMidity	KDE MIDI multimedia player
tn3270	Terminal emulator for IBM mainframes
UFS	UNIX File System
unix2dos	Command to convert UNIX text files to MS-DOS text files (man unix2dos)
up2date	Red Hat tool to update RPMs
URL	Uniform Resource Locator
VIDIX	VIDeo Interface for *niX
VMS	Operating system developed by Digital Equipment Corporation

VMware	Virtual machine ware (http://www.vmware.com)
VOIP	Voice over IP
VPN	Virtual Private Network
VRML	Virtual Reality Modeling Language
vt400	Terminal emulator protocol developed by Digital Equipment Corporation
WAV	Microsoft Wave multimedia format
WAX	Windows media format
WEBDAV	Web-based Distributed Authoring and Versioning
WebEx	Web-based meeting and training tool (http://www.webex.com)
Wine	Linux-based tool for emulating Windows (http://www.winehq.com)
WMA	Windows Media format
WMV	Windows Media format
WMX	Windows Media format
WP	WordPerfect 5.1 document
WVX	Windows Media format
XCF	GIMP image format
xchat	IRC client (man xchat)
xdvi	X viewer for DVI files
xfig	X figure drawing tool (man xfig)
xine	MultiMedia player (http://xinehq.de)
xkeycaps	Graphical client to modify the X keyboard mapping (http://www.jwz.org/xkey-caps)
XLB	Microsoft Excel document
XLS	Microsoft Excel document
xmms	X MultiMedia System (man xmms)
xmodmap	X tool for modifying the keyboard mapping (man xmodmap)

xpdf	X Portable Document Format viewer (man xpdf)
xterm	X Terminal emulator (man xterm)
Yahoo	Yahoo! instant messaging protocol and network
YaST2	SuSE Linux configuration tool

A

Installation of CrossOver Office

CrossOver Office is easy to install, and there are two methods by which it can be installed: system-wide and user mode. System-wide installation is useful if everyone who logs into the system will use the exact same programs. It is also very useful from a maintenance and control perspective.

CrossOver Office is installed via RPM on most systems.

```
rpm —ivh crossover-pro-4.0.1.i386.rpm
```

CrossOver Office provides its own graphical interface for installing Windows programs into its Wine implementation. For example, here is a simple installation of mIRC.

Launch the tool by selecting *Red Fedora->CrossOver Tools->Office Setup* to bring up the installation tool (Figure A.1)

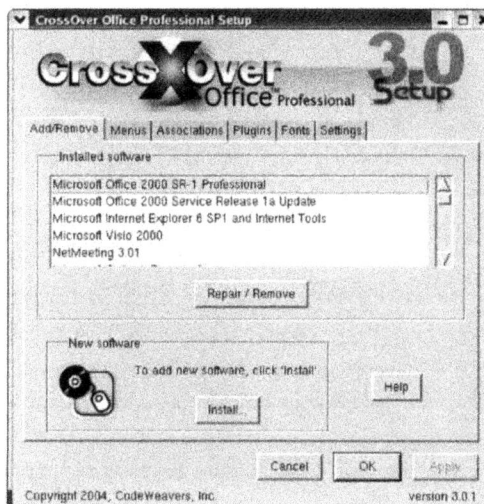

Figure A.1
CrossOver Office installation tool.

Clicking the *Install...* button will bring the installation screen up (Figure A.2).

Figure A.2
*CrossOver Office
"Install Software"
screen.*

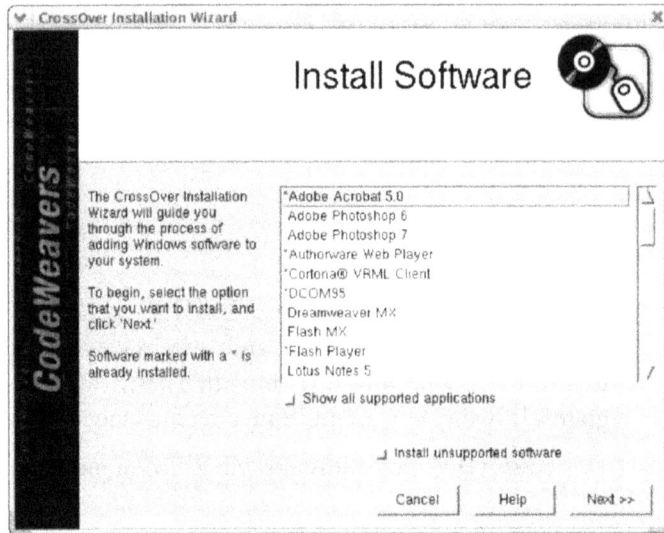

Figure A.2
*CrossOver Office
"Install Software"
screen.*

Check the *Install unsupported software* box and click *Next >>* (Figure A.3).

Figure A.3
*CrossOver Office:
"Install
unsupported
software" box
checked.*

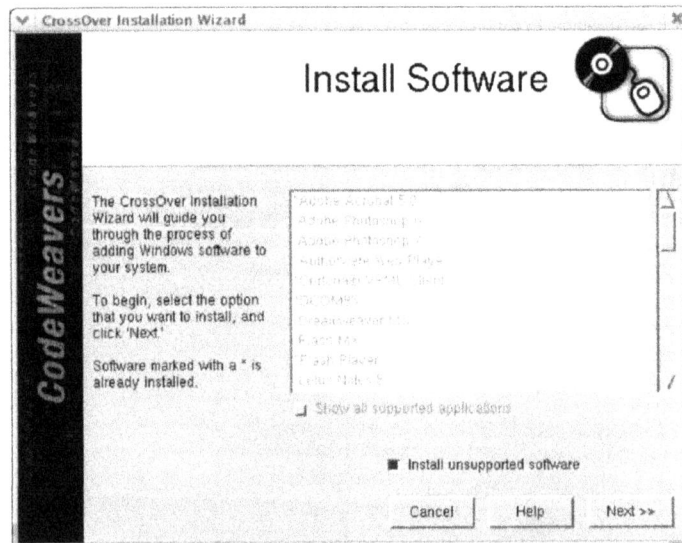

Now, specify the full path to the installation executable for the mIRC program (Figure A.4).

Figure A.4
CrossOver Office
installation tool:
specifying path to
installation
executable for
mIRC.

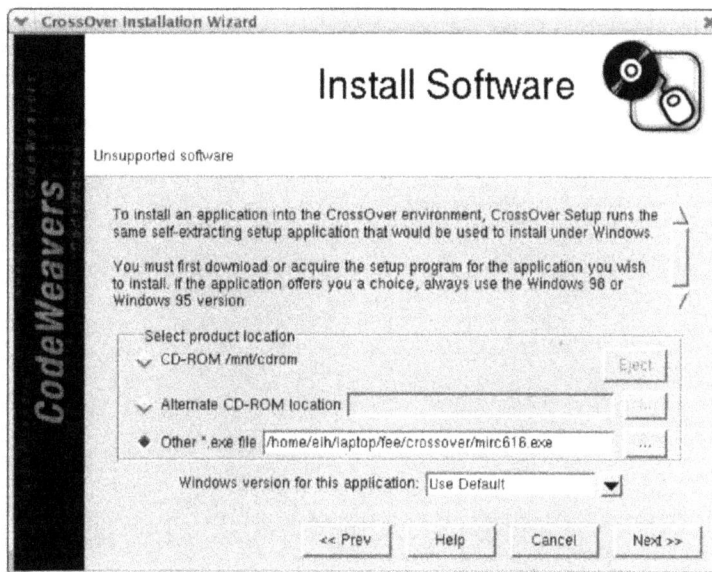

The standard mIRC screens will appear while the CrossOver Office Setup dialog waits for a clean installation of the program (Figure A.5).

Figure A.5
CrossOver Office
installation tool:
installing
unsupported
software.

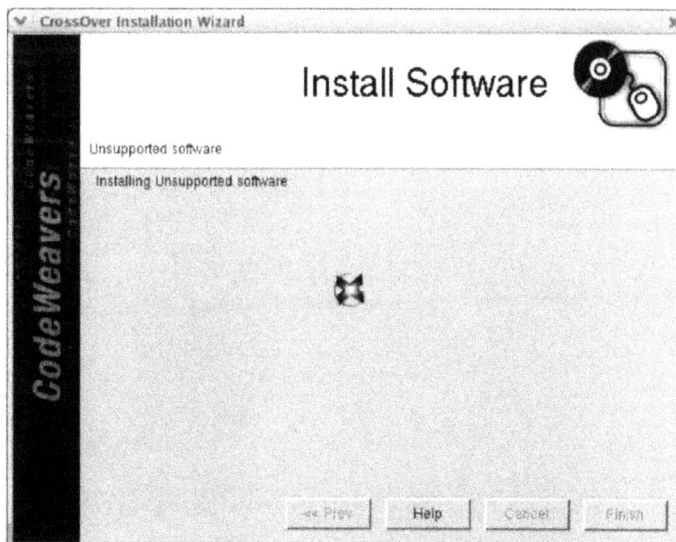

Once the installation is complete, CrossOver Office will bring the Setup dialog back to the first screen, showing the newly installed program.

B

Linux Distributions

There are a myriad of Linux distributions from which to choose for your desktop. Some are specifically designed as a desktop, and others have differing versions of the same base product that support a desktop. The following chart contains a rundown of the various Linux distributions and what makes each one unique. This is only a short list of the most common distributions covered in the book. However, there are a huge number of Linux distributions to meet various needs. These are fully documented at http://www.linux.org/dist/index.html.

Distribution	Comments
Debian	Debian is a great open source distribution of Linux that has nearly everything. However, its base install is still geared toward a single CD-ROM install, with all extra packages available from the Web.
Fedora	Fedora is the non-enterprise track for RedHat. This distribution has a large following and is much more cutting edge than RHEL but with similar functionality.
Mandrake	Mandrake is as full a Linux distribution as can be found; it is geared toward the desktop as well as the server. It is more generic than the enterprise Linux versions of SLES and RHEL. The desktop programs are impressive in their completeness.
Red Hat Enterprise Linux (RHEL)	RHEL provides two server platforms, Advanced Server (AS) and Enterprise Server (ES), as well as a workstation version (WS). Each is different from the others and provides less server functionality with the version changes WS->ES->AS, where AS has the most functionality. Red Hat support is excellent. Red Hat provides a subset of all the possible programs while maintaining supportability.

Distribution	Comments
Slackware	Slackware is still around and contains as much as any other distribution. While it is one of the oldest distributions of Linux, it has maintained a huge following.
SuSE Linux Enterprise Server (SLES)	SLES is mostly a server product, but it can work as a workstation/desktop product as well. Novell owns SuSE and provides excellent support. SuSE also offers a nonenterprise version of its software with less server functionality than SLES. SuSE contains many more programs than Red Hat.
Turbolinux	Turbolinux is geared toward clusters and computational engines.
Ubuntu	Ubuntu, a Debian distribution, provides a simpler and complete user interface with a larger amount of internationalization than any other distribution.

C

Installing WordPerfect

WordPerfect 8 for Linux is no longer available; however, you can still find a copy out on the network as well as public registrations keys at http://linux-mafia.com/wpfaq/downloadwp8.html#REGKEYS. This particular Web site is full of extremely useful data for using WP8 on Linux. What follows is a nutshell installation overview for RHEL3; however, each of the other versions of Linux needs a similar strategy.

1. Before beginning, we must realize that WP8 for Linux was released around the time when Red Hat 5.0 was out. Also, there is no later Linux version available. So we will need some older libraries installed on the system in order to run WP8. The RPMs for these libraries can be found at http://www.rpmfind.net by searching for ld.so and libc. The RPMs required are ld.so-1.9.5-5.i386.rpm and libc-5.3.12-28.i386.rpm and are part of the Red Hat 5.0 Update series of RPMs. These RPMs will install just fine on a RHEL3 and RHEL4 system and will NOT affect the running of newer applications, since these libraries and tools do not overwrite any existing library tools.

2. After the installation of the libraries, we can continue with the install of WP8 by first unpackaging the compressed tar file.

   ```
   tar —xzf wp8.tar.gz
   ```

3. Then run the script Runme and answer the questions with the defaults for your answers. There is an error early on but this can be ignored safely.

   ```
   [root@ruffian wordperfect]# ./Runme
   ```

Did you unzip and untar the files you downloaded? (y/n) y

```
Extracting Files...

  Please Wait ../install.wp: line 103: [: EL: integer
expression expected
  ..
  ...
cat: .wptemp: No such file or directory
cat: .wplist: No such file or directory
cat: shared/license.: No such file or directory
  ...
```

4.   Continue on even with the above error, since it is safe to ignore. For other versions of Linux the error could be different, since it is trying to determine your version of Linux.

5.   Next, we need to accept the license and then enter the installation directory. Something similar to /usr/local/wp8 is suggested.

6.   After the installation directory is selected, choose the type of installation; it is recommended that Full Installation be chosen.

7.   Before the installation starts, the installer will ask if you wish to pattern the install after another installation of WP8. Since this is the first time, it is suggested you select to continue without entering anything.

8.   Now comes the time to tell the installer if you desire to edit your /etc/magic file so that tools will automatically recognize WordPerfect 8 files and launch the appropriate tool to edit them. For the installation it is recommended that you update the magic file. However, it is first best to make a copy, just in case.

9.   Before you complete the installation setup, select the language you will be using. For this demonstration English-US was chosen.

10.   An interesting aspect of the installation is the selection of a printer. Since I do not have any of the listed printers and there is no generic PostScript printer, I selected ASCII Text Printer. This will limit my printing to just text printing, unfortunately. However, other tools can read and print WordPerfect files including word which will run via CrossOver office.

11.   We are now close to the install setup completion, with the selection of the Optional Features. It is recommended that the default be selected and continue.

12. Review the installation options and continue to start the installation.

13. The Installation progress bar will track your installation and when at 100 percent your WP8 install is completed . . . Or is it?

WP8 used to install just fine; I have used it with just about any version of Red Hat starting with Red Hat 5 when it was released. However, with modern versions of Linux, there are now more steps required in order to complete your installation of WP8.

1. Run the command ldconfig as root, to ensure the libraries for WP8 are found.

2. Change the permissions on /usr/i486-linux-libc5-lib directory to allow users access to the necessary libraries. For systems that are locked down this will be required but should be checked nonetheless.

```
chmod 755 /usr/i486-linux-libc5/lib
```

The installation of WP8 is now completed, and you can safely run the /usr/local/wp8/wpbin/xwp program to demonstrate this. The screen shown in Figure C.1 will appear when the installation is successful. While this version of WordPerfect will work on Linux, it is old and outdated. The most recent version of WordPerfect is version 12 and this will only run within a VMware session. While WordPerfect may run within Wine, that is relatively untested.

Figure C.1
Running
WordPerfect 8.

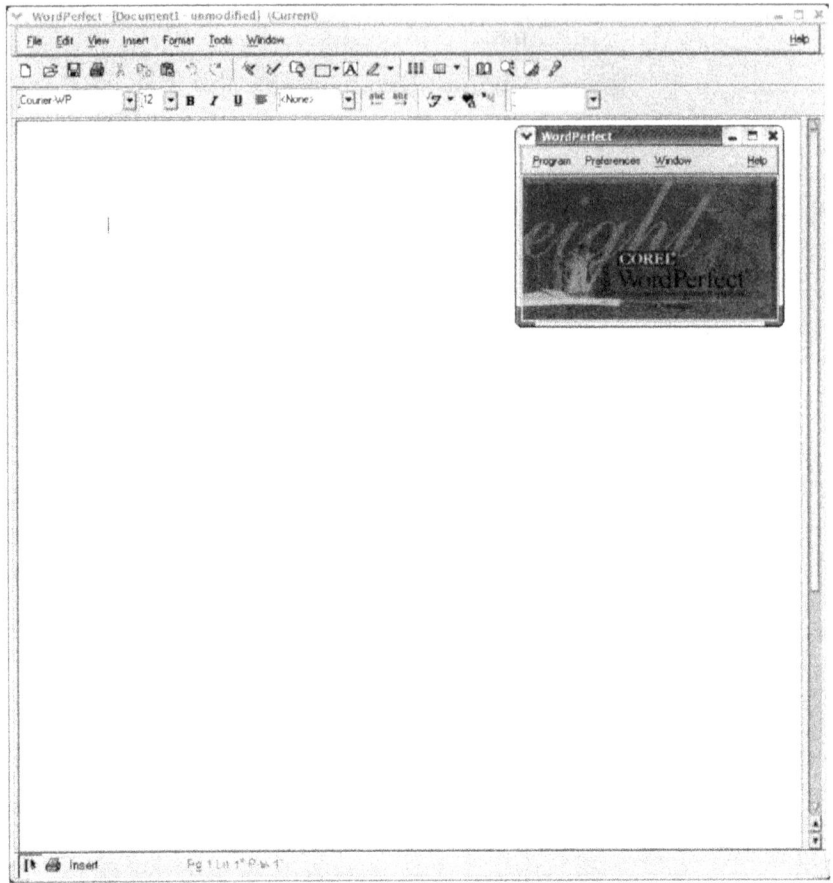

Index

www.ingramcontent.com/pod-product-compliance
Lightning Source LLC
Chambersburg PA
CBHW061414210326
41598CB00035B/6216